#RUSSIAGATE

TRUTH, POST-TRUTH OR DAMNED LIES?

VOL 1

by

Peter Boykin

Everybody hates fake news, right?

Then again, one man's fake news is another man's infallible truth.

So how to discern truth from falsehood, in the foaming churning sea of 'narratives' and 'counter-narratives?'

Ever since the nihilistic professors of chaos undermined public discourse and the very foundations of language, by the 'revolution' of postmodernist nihilism, where everybody has a right to their own opinions and reality is whatever you make of it, the risk that facts, truth and history would be finally reduced to mere 'narratives' has always loomed menacingly upon the horizon. And although the Party of Truth has often striven valiantly against the Party of Feelz, the threat of a purely subjective and emotional approach to the world has made significant inroads.

This being so, it's a truly extraordinary sight to see those who actually *invented* 'post-truth' and 'alternative facts' consistently railing against these very same things. The supposedly impossible election of President Donald J. Trump in November 2016 left the liberal media and the anxious elites scrambling for a way to discredit the legitimately elected President of the United States of America.

And seemingly, the only way they could do so was to project their own falsehoods, fallacies and frailties onto the President, who in turn acted as a surrogate for the despised American working class: the so-called 'Basket of Deplorables,' who yet again were portrayed as ignorant, backward, cousin-loving hicks and rednecks.

Now such contemptibly one-sided stereotyping may well run against the 'Official Narrative' of the liberal elites of the Democratic Party, as to what they really stand for. But it most certainly does not in any contradict their time-honored 'practices.'

For these, in fact, are notoriously hypocritical. From the racially motivated lynching of the Vietnamese American Andy Ngo by Antifa (on the grounds of a perceived lack of intellectual purity, surprise surprise!) to the constant hounding of Candace Owens, Justice Clarence Thomas and Thomas Sowell as 'Uncle Toms,' liberal progressivism has not been short of regressive attitudes more worthy of their notorious antebellum counterparts, when the Democratic Party was associated more with being stone cold comatose at the wheel of racial equality than with wokeness.

No wonder, then, that those Americans who have decided to #WalkAway from the Democratic Plantation are either stigmatized or ignored: in order to perpetuate the fake news 'narrative' that Trump supporters are just old, bitter, impoverished, irresponsible, feckless, shiftless, immoral, angry white males.

But in fact, the Trump movement has captured the imagination of people across whole sectors of the United States of America; because after all, if America is not a nation of shared values, it's hard to see what it could possibly be.

And yet, in order to better peddle their usual Orange Man Bad fake news narrative, the mainstream media, wholly in thrall as they are to the usual elitist, out of touch 'revolving door' establishment interests, there is a constant thrust to perpetually obsess over racism, both real and imagined; while Trump's Rainbow Coalition, by the same token, must ever be either dismissed, mischaracterized, attacked or simply passed over; in a silence every bit as crushingly complicit as it is unspeakably ridiculous!

In such a context, where the noonday sun of populist truth is menaced by the midnight gloom of aristocratic falsehood, and the dusk of integrity grimly heralds forth the dawn of MSM lies, it's comforting to remember how we've been here before.

Many, many times.

Because after all:

America has always, and always will be, at least as this side of the grave and of eternity is concerned, a work in progress. But it is still a tremendous project.

And no amount of 'America was Never that Great' comments from the Andrew Cuomos of this world will ever be able to change that.

And it's not surprising that in the face of such rampant wowzerism, combined with the customary 'post-truth' attitudes of the mainstream media and the liberal elites, that Russiagate emerged as one of the most ridiculous cases of mass hysteria and paranoia, if not outright psychosis, in the history of our tremendous nation...

CONTROLLING THE NARRATIVE

The scandalous critic and writer, Voltaire, once said that if God did not exist, he would have to be invented! The same, however, can be said of Russiagate.

If there were no Russiagate, that would be all the more reason to provide some 'post-truth' and 'alternative facts.' We're all going to have to have a think about who might be responsible for the Russiagate hoax. But first of all, we need to look through the events of Russiagate. Because only when we know the *real* facts, not the *alternative facts*, can we finally begin any serious reflections on the Russiagate scam.

Hopefully, one day, there will be a proper legal investigation to properly apportion blame. But for now, there are no laws against thought!

After all, it never stopped the Democrats...

THREE NARRATIVES, ONE DELUSION!

Well, we're now going to have a brief look at three different interpretations of the Russiagate affair.

On May 30, 2019 Stephen F. Cohen wrote an article in The Nation, discussing three very distinct interpretations of how Russiagate started.[i] One of these, i.e. the official or received narrative, runs as follows. A little while before the July 2016 investigation into Donald Trump began, Obama era intelligence officials noted some illicit links between the Trump campaign and officials who were somehow 'linked' to the Russian government.

As Cohen notes, the latter is a very vague notion. Anyway, this official narrative says that intel, acting appropriately on their leads, decided to formally launch an investigation into Trump.

A second view, apparently held by some pro Trump supporters at Fox News and elsewhere, is that the Steele Dossier that made potentially damning accusations about Trump was the *real* Russian plot! Conspiracy upon conspiracy.

The third possibility, which Cohen calls 'Intelgate,' is that Trump was set up by a corrupt political and intelligence establishment.

Which one of these is the more plausible interpretation? Well, as this series proceeds, you can decide for yourself what the most likely scenario is. The main meat of each individual volume is the actual timeline of events.

In Volume 1, the timeline goes as far as the immediate aftermath of Trump's successful election campaign.

In Volume 2, the timeline goes as far as the eruption of the Mueller Report, or rather 'Witch Hunt.'

Volume 3 takes us all the way to 'case closed,' or as Trump rightly calls it: 'No Collusion, No Obstruction!'

Each volume of the series will also have a conclusion which draws some important lessons about this sad and sorry tale of a seemingly *irredeemably* corrupt elite, who are constantly trying their level best to preserve their ill-gotten privileges against an insurgent establishment outsider and the vast army of populists and patriots standing behind Donald Trump's world-renowned America First agenda!

Please note that anything that has been alleged about hacks, phishing and myriad shadowy espionage individuals or groups, like Guccifer, is difficult to obtain any proof about, whether for or against. The references to certain purported cyberattacks should be read with this crucial caveat in mind.

Also, as regards the structure of the timeline: some of the events took place over a considerable period of time, or occasionally, may even be vague in terms of where to locate them on the calendar. This is why the timeline is mainly structured in terms of months, rather than specific dates. The format followed here prizes the readability, and the convenience and coherence of the overall narrative, over strict detail. I trust this will be judged a strength of the book, and not a weakness.

RUSSIAGATE STAGE 1

A NEW DAWN?

Over a year and a half before the November 2016 elections, Donald Trump announces he is making a Presidential Exploratory Committee; this is the first public step towards becoming an upcoming Presidential candidate for the Republican Party. He is destined to face fierce opposition from fellow Republicans who doubt his authenticity as a real Republican.

But how hard can this really be?

In a war-weary population who are just absolutely sick of the status quo?

Jeb Bush, the brother of former presidents George W Bush and son of Herbert Walker Bush (George Bush Sr.), will defend the legacy of his family and their robust foreign policy interventionism, apparently finding it hard to take Trump seriously (just look at his face in the Presidential debates!)

Then there's Ted Cruz, the archetypical rugged, straight-shooting Texas Republican, who seriously questions Trump's conservative credentials. According to Cruz, Trump's heart is *actually* with the shallow 'New York Values' of empty materialism and liberal social perspectives; and not with a more traditional conservative vision. Then Marco Rubio gets a little weeny bit angry...

Well OK, I guess they all do a bit!

And everyone is looking to the future: because the long-range view is key. So, in this context, it's maybe not surprising to see a certain widely viewed satirical animation here: The Simpsons! This satirical cartoon had prophesied the rise of Trump, and it may well be that the writers of this program, like the mainstream, thought the idea too ludicrous to even be seriously entertained![ii]

But then again, history is kinda funny like that...

OUT WITH THE OLD, IN WITH THE NEW!

FAST-FORWARD JUNE 2015:

NO MORE CAN-KICKING

On June 16, 2015, Trump formally announces his candidacy, and quickly makes waves with his controversial statements and fiery rhetoric: illegal immigrants and Islam are two of the biggest hot-button topics. He mocks his fellow candidates for not being able to take the heat; and worse still, for missing their aircon:

How are they going to beat ISIS? I don't think it's gonna happen.

He also stirs the restless bones of the old (not so) Sleeping Dragon:

When was the last time anybody saw us beating, let's say, China in a trade deal? They kill us. I beat China all the time. All the time.

Even a close ally (albeit deadly rival within close memory) suffers a blow from this renewed trading rivalry:

When did we beat Japan at anything? They send their cars over by the millions, and what do we do? When was the last time you saw a Chevrolet in Tokyo?

Mexico comes next:

> *When do we beat Mexico at the border? They're laughing at us, at our stupidity. And now they are beating us economically.*

Trump then continues:

> *When Mexico sends its people, they're not sending their best. They're not sending you. They're not sending you. They're sending people that have lots of problems, and they're bringing those problems with us. They're bringing drugs. They're bringing crime. They're rapists. And some, I assume, are good people.*
>
> *But I speak to border guards and they tell us what we're getting! And it only makes common sense. It only makes common sense… They're sending us not the right people.*

Now while Trump's rhetoric was merely inflammatory to some, if not downright racist, in others it struck a serious chord of longing. A sense that something was missing; one subtle, deadly whiff that there was just something really inauthentic about the current period of American history.

A deadly whiff.

Deadly for the elites, elected and unelected alike…
Meanwhile, Trump shares a Breitbart article[iii] from renowned American conservative, David Horowitz on his Twitter[iv] and Facebook[v] accounts. The article is entitled 'Donald Trump's speech is a Game-Changer,' and Trump's Facebook share simply says:

> *In order to make America SAFE - we cannot be politically correct!*

Jeffrey Guterman, who by now is one of the most devoted anti-Trump trolls, was first in line to take the bait.[vi]

Thank you for posting this article by David Horowitz, @realDonaldTrump. Please do not change for anybody. #MakeAmericaGreatAgainForEveryone!

A little twee perhaps, given that politics necessary involves conflicts of interest: legitimate migrants versus illegal aliens, law-abiding patriotic Muslims versus jihadists.

And even now, as of June 2019, post-Mueller report, he is still having fun.

Responding to a pro Trump account who called him a douche, Guterman responds:[vii]

I am a douche? Well, at least I have been near a vagina.

Well, I guess we'll just have to take his word for it, huh?!
Another borderline edgy tweet, which we can only hope pure satire(-ish), was:[viii]

Twitter Live #Periscope I'm consulting mental health pros about placing tRump involuntarily in psychiatric facility (sic)

Well, let's just hope Trump Derangement Syndrome (TDS) isn't in the handbook any time soon…
But back to 2016!

Some pleasingly honestly-entitled 'Spin Doctor' says:[ix]

Your unfavorables in new ABC/Post poll: Blacks 94% Hispanics 89% Women 77% Under 50 76% College grads 74% Adult 70% Ind 68%.

This 'bad numbers' meme would go on to be a key meme for the

Fake News Industrial Complex, or FNIC. One particularly funny meme was CNN's triumphant (not to say triumphalist!) election month declaration that Hillary's chances of winning had just swung up from an already-high 78% to as much as 91%![x]

Or again, there is one particular intellectual from the leftist thinkie-journal, Vox, who warns Trump as follows:[xi]

> *You're right! Polls indicate it was so reprehensible that the game is basically over. Sad!*

Angry television celebrity Mo Collins (sorry, temporarily incandescent with unbridled liberal rage television celebrity Mo Collins) shrieked:[xii]

> *That FACE is a game changer!! Ive got a suggestion as to where you can stick that thumb! #ass*

One thing at least is clear from the reception of Trump's speech: the elites truly were, and in many cases, still are, against him. By the time of writing, however, it is safe to say he's already made significant inroads.

But as we continue our journey down the dark and wacky rabbit hole of Russiagate, *do* try to bear in mind the relentless hostility of Hollywood actors, West End luvvies, intel creeps, fake news gurus and think tank shills have had towards the Donald right from day one...

SEPTEMBER 2015

An FBI special agent, Adrian Hawkins, tells the DNC some of its computer systems have been hacked by a group linked to the Russian authorities: 'The Dukes.' The DNC apparently don't take this seriously, allegedly because they thought the message might possibly have been a prank.[xiii] Well, this sounds almost as much of a joke as the person who referred to underprivileged young black youths as 'Superpredators' who had to be 'brought to heel,'[xiv] suddenly deciding to accuse Trump of 'racism' for his tough rhetoric on illegal immigration! Trump and Reince Priebus were quick to remind her of this fact: Clinton's memory has proven to be a little unreliable at times anyway; or so it would appear now, anyway!

But either way, this story about the IT system of the 'Superpoliticians' is due to mushroom out of control, as a tidal wave of conspiracy theories from the Democrats and the mainstream media is about to engulf the country. All eyes are finally drawn to America, the blessed City Upon a Hill in a famished desert of globalist despair!

MARCH 2016

Wikileaks have long been a thorn in the side of the establishment. So, what could possibly be more of a spiky thing to do than release over 30 000 emails from the Clinton server, 7,570 of these being from HRC herself; much to the chagrin of the Democrats and the mainstream media?[xv]

We are yet to hear whether they would be quite as offended if a Republican alone had been hacked, but I'll leave this one for a wiser head than mine to unravel.

Still, this is what Wikileaks have said about it:[xvi]

> *On March 16, 2016 WikiLeaks launched a searchable archive for over 30 thousand emails & email attachments sent to and from Hillary Clinton's private email server while she was Secretary of State. The 50,547 pages of documents span from 30 June 2010 to 12 August 2014. 7,570 of the documents were sent by Hillary Clinton. The emails were made available in the form of thousands of PDFs by the US State Department as a result of a Freedom of Information Act request. More PDFs were made available on February 29, 2016, and a set of additional 995 emails was imported up to February 2, 2018.*

Around this time, an operative of the soon-to-be-notorious Russian 'Fancy Bear' collective[xvii] was probing and penetrating the DNC server system. On 19 March 2016, a huge raid using the insidious cyberattack technique of 'spear-phishing'[xviii] results in many thousands of prominent DNC figurehead John Podesta's emails being stolen, with some interesting consequences to ensue later on.

APRIL 2016

Hackers linked to the GU/GRU (Main Directorate of the General Staff of the Armed Forces of the Russian Federation) gain access to the DNC computer network. It is alleged that this apparent hack is actually the second one of its kind; as 'Cozy Bear,' a GRU-affiliated hacker group, penetrated the servers in July 27, 2015. And that was almost a year before any hacked documents were finally released into the public domain.[xix] Hackers also use stolen credentials to infiltrate the *Democratic Congressional Campaign Committee* or DCCC, and install some malware. (If this long-winded alphabet soup name by any chance sounds to you like a Communist organization, I probably wouldn't worry about it. Better not ask too many questions!)[xx]

Also in this month, Obama announces his desire to appoint various new key administration figures.[xxi] Among these is Steven Chabinsky, the general counsel and chief risk officer for Crowd-Strike, who was appointed to the Commission on Enhancing National Cybersecurity.

MAY 2016

Crowdstrike, a (more or less!) 'private' company who actually have links to the FBI, blame the hacking on both Cozy Bear and Fancy Bear, both of which circles are apparently linked to the Russian authorities. Still, thousands more DNC emails are stolen this month!

In this regard, Justin Caruso of the Daily Caller notes some interesting 'inconvenient truths,' if you will![xxii] Aside from the links between Crowdstrike and the Obama administration, it was initially Crowdstrike who examined the DNC servers, not the FBI. Also, the DNC claimed that the FBI never wanted to see the servers, but James Comey went on to flat out contradict them!

There are also some pretty disturbing links to that shady, sinister place where the corporate and intellectual worlds meet: the TTIC or Think Tank Industrial Complex, potentially no less dangerous than the Military-Industrial Complex of which Eisenhower warned as early as 1950, and which has since swollen up to gargantuan proportions, creating an empire that seems almost destined to last forever; well until Trump finally manages to bring it to heel, of course!

Yes: believe it or not, one of the Crowdstrike co-founders, Dmitri Alperovitch, is involved with the highly controversial establishment foreign policy think tank the Atlantic Council, which is steeped in the highly ideological views of foreign policy espoused by Barack Obama, George W Bush, Hillary Clinton and Bill

Clinton. The NATO-funded Atlantic Council perceive Russia to be one of the biggest threats against America. The Atlantic Council also gets funding from the Open Society Initiative for Europe, which is in turn related to the Open Society Foundation of the widely criticized billionaire philanthropist George Soros.

And another funder of the Atlantic Council is the Victor Pinchuk Foundation, named after a billionaire who is alleged to have given $25 million to the Clinton Foundation.

Finally, Crowdstrike itself has received $100 million of investments from Google Capital (later known as Capital G). The latter company is owned by Alphabet; whose chairman, Eric Schmidt, is a huge Clinton supporter, who even wanted to help her campaign in 2016.
But we're not just dealing with potential conflicts of interest here, and the usual revolving door politics.

Actually, we're dealing with basic questions of competency here as well! So, it's just as well we have the UK's prominent conservative tabloid, the Daily Mail, to help us out here.[xxiii] The paper notes that Crowdstrike would be later to have retracted some of their claims from a December 2016 report, owing to their uncritical alliance on the writings of an unnamed person the newspaper calls a 'pro Putin propaganda blogger.'

All in all, questions have to be asked about the impartiality and objectivity of Crowdstrike. Did they have too much skin in the game to behave in an objective and impartial manner?

Is it possible they may have been guided by some kind of bias, even if unconscious? And are they even as competent, serious and professional as we would all like to hope?

An in-depth discussion of all these matters would take a book in itself; but perhaps they are all things we need to think about a little and to bear in mind, going forward.

JUNE 2016

'DCLeaks' and 'Guccifer 2.0,' who the Mueller investigation consider to be GRU conspirators from Russia hiding behind pseudonyms,[xxiv] release another huge stash of stolen emails. The DHS claim there are foreign actors infiltrating voter-registration databases and systems, in order to manipulate them. They claim some breaches have already been made.[xxv]

Sad to hear about this: I mean, when was the last time you heard Obama or other neoliberals trying to interfere in the power structures of other countries?!

...

Oh wait, I almost forgot about Libya![xxvi]

SAD!

Our mutual boss, @POTUS44, launched Operation Inherent Resolve (2 year operation) and bombed Libya without Congressional authorization.[xxvii]

Here's my floor speech from 2011 regarding @POTUS44's unconstitutional war in Libya: http://youtu.be/XsEDLxi45u4 . Please view & share. @POTUS risks making the same mistakes in Syria. The people must speak on war through the votes of their representatives. Our Constitution demands it.[xxviii]

> *Mr. @POTUS44 @BarackObama, please stand up and speak for young African men and women being tortured, killed and sold like goats in LIBYA. I hold you and your (former) administration directly responsible for Libya's aftermath. Cc: @MichelleObama @UN @RailaOdinga @POTUS'*[xxix]

Obama's legacy has been a complete disaster, including his meddling in the affairs of other countries; a long standing tendency Trump is gradually wearing down, via the demoralization of the enemy and the spread of alternative ideas; not abroad only, but at home as well!

And yes: the *real* threat to democracy is not Trump and his alleged conspiracy with Russia, but rather those who place American lives in danger with reckless foreign adventurism. The behavior of George Bush Junior, Barack Obama and the Clinton dynasty, among others, is a simply heartbreaking blot upon our amazing country. But when we stand together as one country, of every creed and color, on the basis of the shared values that made us all great, and not on the reckless hubris of a world-imperial mission, then bad ideas and actors, home or abroad can at most trouble the American spirit; but never once shall they succeed in crushing it!

This very same action-packed month Fusion GPS, a commercial research and strategic intelligence firm, hires Christopher Steele to investigate the Trump team. Steele is a former agent of the shadowy British intel collective, MI6: roughly equivalent to the CIA, as it focuses on foreign rather than domestic intelligence. Bit of context here: MI6 got an unfavorable mention in the Chilcot Report on the Iraq War for their endearingly naïve and impressionable reliance on the 'fake news,' or rather 'fake intel,' that lay behind the Iraq War dossier.[xxx]

Worth noting in passing that UK intel, like the USA, have had their fair share of scandals: for example, MI6's sister organization, MI5 (domestic, not foreign intelligence) have the right to break the law in order to achieve their goals.[xxxi]

This is reminiscent of the old conspiracy theory in Europe, where they used to falsely claim the Jesuits had a 'white letter' or 'carte blanche' to absolve them in advance of any terrible crime or treasonous act.

When news about this broke in March 2018, there was of course zero attempt to provide transparency about what this meant.

US intelligence itself, some would say, has its own *transparency issues…'*

Well speaking of which, the controversial 35 page Steele dossier, or 'Pissgate Dossier,' later published by Buzzfeed[xxxii] in January 2017,[xxxiii] is the result of this commission. This tiresome screed has gained notoriety perhaps comparable only to the notorious 'Dodgy Dossier' that the UK authorities used in order to justify war with Iraq, along with the fanciful '45 minutes' claim that was widely derided by opponents of globalism. The Steele Dossier was so ridiculous, that Trump's soon-to-be-disgraced lawyer, Michael Cohen,[xxxiv] sued Buzzfeed.[xxxv]

> *Enough is enough of the #fake #RussianDossier. Just filed a defamation action against @BuzzFeedNews for publishing the lie filled document on @POTUS @realDonaldTrump and me!*

He also made sure to sue Fusion GPS. Later on, he dropped the suits. Some might assume his fear of legal trouble seems to have 'trumped' his loyalty to the President; but rather than going low, the most generous thing we can all say here is that the guy is already a non-entity, so we might as well not give him a hard time about it. He's no Bill Clinton, put it that way…

Or wait, maybe he is!

But Michael Cohen is not the only 'expert' in trouble here. Fusion GPS and Buzzfeed have suffered reputational damage that is perhaps exceeded only by that of ardent Never Trumpers CNN, commonly derided as 'fake news' by many Americans and freedom lovers all over the world, and whose catastrophic decline in ratings has now plumbed dizzying new depths; ever since the Mueller Report told the real truth about their utterly deluded 'Russian Bears under the Bed' anti-Trump conspiracy theories.[xxxvi]

Anyone who either creates or publishes something like the following...

Well, it surely wouldn't be nice to question their integrity, but we certainly have to take a good, hard look at their *sanity!*

> *Former top intelligence officer claims FSB has compromised TRUMP through his activities in Moscow sufficiently to be able to blackmail him. According to several knowledgeable sources, his conduct to Moscow has included perverted sexual acts which have been arranged/monitored by the FSB.*

So the FSB brought him all the way to a hotel in Moscow, just to circle-jerk while they say a Russian prostitute, and/or agent, started getting'-pissy-wit-it?

Sure. Cool story, bro!

As for the reference to Trump's alleged 'personal obsessions and sexual frustrations,' the very premise of 'Pissgate' raises the odd question or two about whether there is any Freudian projection going on here.

Not to mention outright delusional behavior! In a fantastic LSD flourish that would make the Aladdin-addled Iraq War dossier scribblers (maybe the primary source for their magic fairy weapons and nasty Arab villain WMD delusions were those well-beloved Disney movies?), we find out:

> *The hotel was known to be under FSB control with microphones and concealed cameras in all the main rooms to record anything they wanted to.*

Not so much George Orwell, as George bloody Harrison, at the very height of his psychedelic powers!

So we'll just let the President have the last word here:[xxxvii]

FAKE NEWS - A TOTAL POLITICAL WITCH HUNT!

Well now, look at this. A little bit late in the day? The DNC, or so the story runs, manage to get rid of the hackers; who may well have had access for over a year by now. The DNC publicly accuse Russia of making this breach. Around this time, the campaign of Marco Rubio, as well as the Republican Party's equivalent of the DNC, the RNC, undergo an 'attempted breach' (Time Magazine)[xxxviii] or perhaps one that may be successful, but we just don't know how successful (Daily Beast).[xxxix]

And what about Trump's campaign?

Well, Cryin' James Comey of the Never Trump FBI (of which more later) went on to claim, in 2017, that there was no evidence of the Russians trying to hack Trump's campaign.

How convenient…

Well I guess that's settled then, isn't it!

After all, it's the FBI, so it must be true, right?!

Well, we soon find out that 'Guccifer 2.0' takes credit for the hacks, and also sends the flamboyant media muckrakers[xl] Gawker[xli] a leaked file of anti-Trump opposition research; also contacting The Smoking Gun as well.[xlii] Wikileaks and Guccifer 2.0 communicate on Twitter (via Direct Messaging); because if Wikileaks get some documents, as it will have an even bigger impact if *they* publish Guccifer's loot. [xliii]

> *[T]hese other media groups are very likely to take a stupid initial angle... We don't know if its true. Possibly russians who knows blah blah blah.' (sic)*

Well, interesting.
The plot thickens...

JULY 2016

Christopher Steele shows an FBI agent some of his findings, which supposedly 'prove' Trump was part of an election conspiracy.[xliv] Guccifer 2.0 releases another huge stash of DNC documents.[xlv]

Meanwhile, Senator Dianne Feinstein and Representative Adam Schiff of the Gang of Eight are sending a letter to Obama about the threat of electoral interference. They are attributing to Crowdstrike the opinion that the FSB and GRU were behind the recent acts of infiltration.[xlvi]

> *If true, and if Russia made the material available to WikiLeaks for release, then the episode would represent an unprecedented attempt to meddle in American domestic politics—one that would demand a response by the United States.*

Meanwhile, Trump finally manages to become the Republican candidate at last.

And there is, of course, a celebratory tweet:[xlvii]

> *Such a great honor to be the Republican Nominee for President of the United States. I will work hard and never let you down! AMERICA FIRST!*

Meanwhile, the Illinois State Board of Elections suffers hostile cyber activities, ostensibly linked to Russia;[xlviii] and Wikileaks strikes a lucky 7 with as many as 20 000 emails from just over half

a dozen top DNC officials![xlix]
DNC Chairwoman Debbie Wasserman Schultz ends up having to resign over the Wikileaks publications.[l] According to the Clinton campaign, citing conveniently unnamed 'experts,'[li] it was Russian intelligence operators who compromised the e-mails.

Trump goes on to joke that Russia ought to give all Clinton's emails to US intelligence,[lii] and that he hopes Russia[liii] can somehow manage to find the emails.[liv]

> *If Russia or any other country or person has Hillary Clinton's 33,000 illegally deleted emails, perhaps they should share them with the FBI!*

Despite everything, the controversial centrist Clinton wins the Democratic Nomination.[lv] Her most formidable opponent, social democrat Bernie Sanders, didn't prevail in the end,[lvi] although allegations of a nomination system rigged[lvii] against the fiery populist continue to dog[lviii] the Democratic Party[lix] to this day.

AND SO IT BEGINS...

On July 31, 2016, the FBI begin their 'counter-intelligence investigation' into the alleged collusion between Russia and Trump: 'Crossfire Hurricane.'[lx] Meanwhile, CIA Director John Brennan forms a working group from the three intelligence organizations under the Department of Homeland Security or DHS: the Federal Bureau of Investigation (FBI), the Criminal Intelligence Agency (CIA) and the National Security Agency (NSA). Brennan calls it 'an exceptionally, exceptionally sensitive issue.'[lxi]

Hm. Now I wonder what he could possibly have meant by that...?!

AUGUST 2016

Guccifer makes some more dumps; Twitter and WordPress temporarily suspend their accounts. However, the damage is done![lxii]

Trump and Clinton are both warned by the FBI about the threat of Russian interference;[lxiii] the same intelligence organization incites panic over foreign infiltration of election systems in various conveniently unnamed US states.[lxiv] On Sean Hannity's true news show, Julian Assange of Wikileaks ridicules Clinton for her response to the leaks.[lxv]

> *The Democrats are always talking about how horrible McCarthyism was. And it was in many ways. But at least the USSR actually existed then, and there were Russian agents on campaigns in the United States, which was serious.*

> *What we see now is Hillary Clinton and her campaign trying to whip up a neo-McCarthyist hysteria. She claims effectively that Donald Trump and WikiLeaks are agents of the Russians, and her campaign has also implied that Jill Stein, the Green Party leader and The Intercept, a U.S. publication, are agents of the Russians.*

Clinton is not the only one having problems. At the end of the month, many documents from House Minority Leader Nancy Pelosi are compromised by Guccifer. Brennan briefs the bipartisan establishment 'Gang of Eight' on the alleged links between Trump's campaign and Russia. The Gang of Eight are individuals from both major parties who are permitted to receive certain high-security intelligence briefings.

SEPTEMBER 2016

In a secret CIA briefing to congressional leaders, prominent Republican figure Mitch McConnell[lxvi] casts doubt on the allegations of Russian interference.[lxvii]

> *I don't believe they interfered… Could be Russia. And it could be China. And it could be some guy in his home in New Jersey.*

More exciting still: in one of the most notorious and widely discussed text message exchanges of all time, FBI agent Lisa Page texts fellow FBI agent Peter Strzok to plot some talking points for Comey to give to Obama:

> *To know everything we are doing.*

They also call Trump:

> *A fucking idiot.*

Another choice pick is the characterization of Virginians voting against Jill McCabe's Senate campaign (the wife of FBI Deputy Director Andrew McCabe) 'ignorant hillbillys' (sic).[lxviii]

Conspiracy theories are already dogging the Trump team. Publicity manager Kellyanne Conway rebuffs accusations that Carter Page, accused of links to Russia, is acting on Trump's initiative, and downplays his importance as a minor figure in Trump's campaign.[lxix]

Future Obama/Clinton style viral autobiography writer and current FBI director James Comey testifies that by now, even more voter registration databases have seen suspicious activity.[lxx] The authorities must now decide how to respond to his allegations.

Who is really in charge in America? Or is anyone?

OCTOBER 2016

A group of FBI agents meet Christopher Steele, who gives them a second dossier of allegations, this time one composed by Cody Shearer.[lxxi] The 'Peegate' allegations are repeated from the earlier Steele: where Trump is supposedly urinated upon by Kompromat-crazy Russian agents in a 'golden shower' fetish move.

Sounds a bit weird, but OK!

On 7 October, a report from the DHS and ODNI (Office of the Director of National Intelligence) blame Russia for the recent leaks: [lxxii]

> These thefts and disclosures are intended to interfere with the US election process. Such activity is not new to Moscow—the Russians have used similar tactics and techniques across Europe and Eurasia, for example, to influence public opinion there.

However, they also argue:

> The USIC and the Department of Homeland Security (DHS) assess that it would be extremely difficult for someone, including a nation-state actor, to alter actual ballot counts or election results by cyber attack or intrusion. This assessment is based on the decentralized nature of our election system in this country and the number of protections state and local election officials have in place.

Now while we're on the topic of inflammatory activities in

cyberspace, Wikileaks then begin to release thousands of Podesta's emails![lxxiii] Among these are various closed-door speech Clinton had given to Wall Street and bankers in other areas such as Brazil: one so damning, that in an article the very same month, even the establishment liberal newspaper the New York Times spoke drily of a Clinton, in the words of the headline:[lxxiv]

> *At ease with Wall Street.*

Amy Chozick, Nicholas Confessore and Michael Barbaro began with the fact that it was a shadowy closed door meeting that was not disclosed to the public; and immediately proceeded to note how Clinton had courted big business, embraced radical trade and shown an attitude that was less than resoundingly supportive of social security. She also had her very own 'I have a dream' moment, speaking in flamboyant terms about:

> *A hemispheric common market, with open borders, sometime in the future.*

Despite her common campaign tactic of accusing Trump of flagrant dishonesty, she also admitted to having both:

> *Public and private positions.*

Something which, surprisingly enough, doesn't seem much of a vote winner to most Americans…
Another 'quiet bit loud' quote was that she was coming increasingly distant from the middle class as she and her family got wealthier. Lamenting the plight of wealthy people who serve in government, she said:

> *There is such a bias against people who have led successful and/or complicated lives.*

As one final, crushing, self-indignity, she prematurely compares herself to the legendary Democrat Teddy Roosevelt; someone who unlike Clinton, is a figure of world renown; and indeed, who is one of only four national leaders in the entire history of America to find himself worthy of being carved on Mount Rushmore.

But the stupidity and arrogance doesn't stop there!

In the third and final Presidential debates, Clinton goes low and says not only that Russia is behind the DNC leaks, but that Trump is his 'puppet' who is being dangled on a string by the wicked puppet master Vladimir Putin, the strongman Russian leader who Trump is only too willing to cravenly serve.[lxxv]

Of course, Trump points out that she is the 'real puppet.' Presumably, this is because many in America and beyond consider her to be a slave to corporate interests.

This presidential debate with Trump, actually the final one she has with him, involves the notorious '17 agencies' claim, where in a momentary lapse of sanity, she thought there were not only three intelligence agencies alleging Russian collusion, but an imaginary 14 non-existent agencies on top of that![lxxvi]

Then, as Trump claims that it is Clinton who is the real puppet, Clinton continues with her deluded ravings, with perhaps the very best quote of the night:

> It's pretty clear you won't admit that the Russians have engaged in cyberattacks against the United States of America, that you encouraged espionage against our people, that you are willing to spout the Putin line, sign up for his wish list, break up NATO, do whatever he wants to do, and that you continue to get help from him, because he has a very clear favorite in this race.
>
> So I think that this is such an unprecedented situation. We've never had a foreign government trying to interfere in our elec-

> *tion. We have 17 -- 17 intelligence agencies, civilian and military, who have all concluded that these espionage attacks, these cyber-attacks, come from the highest levels of the Kremlin and they are designed to influence our election. I find that deeply disturbing.*

All this dashing use of figures from someone who, according to the paid speeches discussed on Wikileaks, really does seem to believe numbers are a pretty important part of all our lives! I guess it's no surprise then that she's got fixated on facts and figures once again.
Still, what an utterly bizarre person…

Now, as if things couldn't get worse for the person Trump has widely derided as 'Crooked Hillary,' the FBI publicly announce they are re-opening Clinton's email investigation.[lxxvii] There is a long-running tradition for HRC and her supporters to inappropriately trivialize[lxxviii] and wave away[lxxix] her improper use of an unsecured private server for government business, which her critics consider to be an inexcusable abuse of office; if not, indeed, an insidious cover for some kind of unknown, nefarious purposes.

Even Comey of the Never Trump FBI said this:

> *Although we did not find clear evidence that Secretary Clinton or her colleagues intended to violate laws governing the handling of classified information, there is evidence that they were extremely careless in their handling of very sensitive, highly classified information.*

Worse still, the original said, 'grossly negligent;' but Comey's notorious Peter Strzok changed it to 'extremely careless!'[lxxx]

The original wording is more damning; but then again, so is Strzok's deeply disturbing act of interference as well. Could it be that there are some intended legal implications in this shift of language?

Democratic Senate Minority Leader Harry Reid asks Comey to investigate Trump's alleged links to Russia.[lxxxi] However, curiously enough, he doesn't mention a single word about the Priory of Sion, the Society of Jesus, the Illuminati and the Cosmic Lizard Men of David Icke. Maybe next time???

Meanwhile, Obama makes a stunning revamp of his 'Red Line' braggadocio over Syria, an idle threat to President Assad over civilian casualties. The latter, of course, was a notoriously empty rhetorical gesture that was widely panned by media critics and Twitter users. It does of course sit cutely enough alongside his disastrous comparison of the bloodthirsty Islamic State/ISIL/Daesh/Artist-Formerly-Known-as-ISIS as a 'Jayvee Team' who, in a stunning bout of Dunning-Kruger Syndrome, seemed to think they were the Los Angeles Lakers; when they were in fact a few incompetent and inexperienced bad guys who just got lucky!
Not unlike a lot of the Democrats and fake news gurus of today...

So what is Obama going to do about it?

No idea!

And that's precisely the point now, isn't it?

One anonymous source so beloved of the mainstream media, a 'senior administration official,' says the following:[lxxxii]

> *The president has made it clear that we will take action to protect our interests, including in cyberspace, and we will do so at a time and place of our choosing. Consistent with the practice we have adopted in the past, the public should not assume that they will necessarily know what actions have been taken or what actions we will take.*

Wowee! Sounds a bit like Syria, doesn't it…
Stunning stuff!

Meanwhile, allegations abound that election officials are being targeted by the GRU in Florida, the land of Walt Disney![lxxxiii]

Oh and speaking of a Disneyfied view of the world, the 'Never-Trump' FBI go wayyyyy down the Fantasy Island rabbit hole, scaremongering about how at least one county government's web network ended up vulnerable enough to be subject to foreign manipulation; cool headed state officials in Florida, however, deign to demur.[lxxxiv]

After months of seemingly letting their guard down on cyber-security to an unprecedented degree, a bunch of Angry Democrats complain to the FBI about a mysterious Aladdin-style magic device outside the DNC offices, Washington that can somehow intercept mobile phone calls.[lxxxv]

However, this mysterious Jaffar-like weapon of mass magical distraction goes the way of Saddam's WMDs, as even the potentially compromised FBI can find nothing!

Meanwhile, some snowflake anonymous DNC source told prominent liberal news magazine Mother Jones:[lxxxvi]

> *We are the oldest political party in this country, and we are under constant attack from Russia and/or maybe others.*

Sounds like somebody needs a safe space, huh?!

It is, however, interesting to note that the Democrats seem to think they are the only people under attack… Perhaps Republicans are just being stoic about any attacks directed at them? Or maybe they're just putting proper cybersecurity procedures in to begin with? Just a thought...[lxxxvii]

On 8 November 2016, Trump finally wins the election! Hillary Clinton's notorious 'basket of deplorables' gaffe from the previous September seems to have cost her greatly outside of the LA/San Francisco/Las Vegas/Seattle/New York/Washington liberal bubble.[lxxxviii]

> *Y'know, just to be grossly generalistic, you could put half of Trump's supporters into what I call the basket of deplorables. Right? The racist, sexist, homophobic, xenophobic, Islamophobic... You name it! And unfortunately, there are people like that... And he has lifted them up! He has given voice to their websites that used to only have 11,000 people – now have 11 million. He tweets and retweets their offensive, hateful, mean-spirited rhetoric. Now, some of those folks – they are irredeemable. But thankfully... they are not America!*

This, on top of decades of sleaze, and the general sense of disgust and 'dynasty fatigue' commonly directed towards prominent political families like the Clintons, led to a clear victory for Trump. Some Clinton supporters thought it was in the bag, and so it was really something to see the look of gathering horror on the faces of the liberal media as Trump inched closer and closer to victory on the night. Even Edgy Alpha Males and Bernie Bros like Cenk Uygur of The Young Turks alternative news outlet were transfixed in wide-eyed horror. But this was Trump's night... And America's!

Evil, however, never sleeps...

DECEMBER 2016

Finally! Flamboyantly irritable Gang of Eight and ardent Never-Trumper John McCain gives the highly suspect Steele dossier to FBI chief Comey. But what happens next?[lxxxix]

Here's what happens next. Fantasy novels, no matter how exciting they may be, are simply not true. And the same is true of Reality Fan-Fic! Whether it's the Kremlin's pissing prostitutes or Saddam's magic disappearing WMDs (anybody see Jaffar yet?!), a whole Gadarene legion of confused genies of delusion somehow never manage to break the intrepid Trump's Aladdin-like courage. The Trump team brush off accusations of Russian interference, reminding everyone that the very people making such hysterical McCarthyite accusations also bought into Bush's deluded nonsense about Saddam's magic disappearing WMDs.[xc]

Well, you'd expect Clinton to take advantage of Trump's discomfort and claim the moral high ground, right?

Or, maybe you wouldn't.

Well, anyway, she doesn't!

Clinton addresses a group of Democrat supporters, telling them Putin has a 'personal beef' against her, on account of her impugning the fairness of the 2011 Russian elections. Clinton seems to have something of a fixation on rigged elections; but that's not her only obsession! She also seems to have an obsession with Russia that is due to grip much of the country in an ever-growing crescendo of deluded hysteria and strident outrage.[xci]

Sore loser, exhibit B! In his final press conference as president before he has a chance to join the Clinton/Blair style merry go round of lucrative speeches, Obama says:[xcii]

Not much happens in Russia without Vladimir Putin.

Was Obama simply grandstanding again as usual, and trying to bring a bit of epic showmanship in with another flamboyant turn of phrase? Or was he trying to simply get all the benefits of accusing Putin, with none of the costs?

You decide!

Still butthurt about losing the election, Obama signs Executive Order 13757. This document focuses on five collective entities from Russia, along with four specific individuals. The groups are as follows:

1. Main Intelligence Directorate (a.k.a. Glavnoe Razvedy-vatel'noe Upravlenie) (a.k.a. GRU); Moscow, Russia.

2. Federal Security Service (a.k.a. Federalnaya Sluzhba Bezo-pasnosti) (a.k.a FSB).

3. Special Technology Center (a.k.a. STLC, Ltd. Special Technology Center St. Petersburg).

4. Zorsecurity (a.k.a. Esage Lab).

5. Autonomous Noncommercial Organization 'Professional Association of Designers of Data Processing Systems' (a.k.a. ANO PO KSI).

The individuals specifically named are all from Russian military intelligence:

1. Igor Valentinovich Korobov

2. Sergey Aleksandrovich Gizunov.

3. Igor Olegovich Kostyukov.

4. Vladimir Stepanovich Alexseyev.[xciii]

The National Cybersecurity and Communications Integration Center (NCCIC), which is part of DHS, or the Department of Homeland Security, releases a report called 'GRIZZLY STEPPE – Russian Malicious Cyber Activity.'[xciv]

This NCCIC report does of course echo DHS and ODNI the report of the previous October. According to this report:

The RIS (Russian civilian and military intelligence services) have part of an ongoing campaign of cyber-enabled operations directed at the U.S. government and its citizens. These cyber operations have included spearphishing campaigns targeting government organizations, critical infrastructure entities, think tanks, universities, political organizations, and corporations leading to the theft of information. In foreign countries, RIS actors conducted damaging and/or disruptive cyber-attacks, including attacks on critical infrastructure networks. In some cases, RIS actors masqueraded as third parties, hiding behind false online personas designed to cause the victim to misattribute the source of the attack.

It's a little embarrassing to learn, however, that the CIA also has the capacity to spoof attacks...

Let's hope they've never had a chance to use them yet![xcv]

UMBRAGE

The CIA's hand crafted hacking techniques pose a problem for the agency. Each technique it has created forms a 'fingerprint' that can be used by forensic investigators to attribute multiple different attacks to the same entity.

This is analogous to finding the same distinctive knife wound on multiple separate murder victims. The unique wounding style creates suspicion that a single murderer is responsible. As soon one murder in the set is solved then the other murders also find likely attribution.

The CIA's Remote Devices Branch's UMBRAGE group collects and maintains a substantial library of attack techniques 'stolen' from malware produced in other states including the Russian Federation.

With UMBRAGE and related projects the CIA cannot only increase its total number of attack types but also misdirect attribution by leaving behind the 'fingerprints' of the groups that the attack techniques were stolen from.

UMBRAGE components cover keyloggers, password collection, webcam capture, data destruction, persistence, privilege escalation, stealth, anti-virus (PSP) avoidance and survey techniques.

Given the stunning Vault 7 revelations above, you have to wonder whether some of the leaked capabilities of US intel have anything to do with Russiagate?

Nobody knows for sure, but it does give you pause for thought... *Doesn't it?!*[xcvi]

Meanwhile, top Putin supporter Lavrov is out for blood after the US sanctions; figuratively speaking of course! But there's trouble in paradise, or at least in Moscow, as Putin goes against Lavrov's advice.[xcvii] A controversial Trump tweet is like red meat to the baying hordes of Never-Trumpers:[xcviii]

> *Great move on delay (by V. Putin) - I always knew he was very smart!*

Instead of treating the tweet as a veiled threat to Putin, the usual liberal and closet-liberal Never Trumpers came out in droves. [xcix]

DNC member Khary Penebaker snarls:[c]

> *Y'all thought you were slick didn't you @realDonaldTrump! Your fanboying of #Putin was a dead giveaway. #TreasonsGreetings #Resist*

Peter Daou grouches thusly:[ci]

> *Shorter Trump:*
> *The White House and congressional leaders from both parties don't have the guts to do sh*t about this.*

Well, talk about an 'Angry Democrat!'

Former CIA ops officer and old-school GOP policy director Evan McMullin rants:[cii]

> *To be clear, @realDonaldTrump is siding with America's greatest adversary even as it attacks our democracy. Never grow desensitized to this.*

And as late as 22 July 2018, angry Andrew Weinstein was still crying about this, saying:[ciii]

> *Barack Obama expelled 35 Russian diplomats and sanctioned nine individuals and entities in December 2016. You responded 2 days later by praising Vladimir Putin for his restraint and called him very smart.*

Oh, the pain!
We just can't bear it anymore!

A true public intellectual as always, Obama follows the time honored neoliberal strategy of listening to the kind of opinions that make you wonder whether the evidence leads to the conclusion, or the conclusion is just the pretext for the evidence.

This new development in the ongoing anti-Trump hate campaign also include two Senate hearings.

And it just so happens that Trump is to get an intel meeting too; a meeting *the very day after* Obama. Hm… ?!
Well, your guess is as good as mine![civ]

Of course, by this point, both the CIA and the FBI are claiming Russia was behind Trump's election victory; even though, years later, Trump was to point out that he helped himself win and didn't need any help from Russia!

Well, Trump may have made himself win. But the CIA and FBI aren't helping much! However, they're arguably not helping their own cause much either…

As they start with a classic hedge!

Assessing Russian Activities and Intentions in Recent US Elections' is a declassified version of a highly classified assessment that has been provided to the President and to recipients approved by the President.

> *The Intelligence Community rarely can publicly reveal the full extent of its knowledge or the precise bases for its assessments, as the release of such information would reveal sensitive sources or methods and imperil the ability to collect critical foreign intelligence in the future.*
>
> *Thus, while the conclusions in the report are all reflected in the classified assessment, the declassified report does not and cannot include the full supporting information, including specific intelligence and sources and methods.[cv]*

As with so much of this story, we truly walk by faith alone!

Oh, and by the way, the report ends with these chilling words...

> *We assess Moscow will apply lessons learned from its campaign aimed at the US presidential election to future influence efforts in the United States and worldwide, including against US allies and their election processes.*

Better duck under the covers...

BIG MOSCOW IS WATCHING YOU...

Unfortunately, however, it all gets rather more personal than that. A general report is one thing, but it came as a surprise to precisely not one person in America (or outside of it!) that US intel sent their boys to heavy Trump in New York. Or at least, maybe they didn't heavy him. Maybe they just gave him a bit of a friendly warning? It would be great to be a fly on the wall for a meeting of such national and world historical significance; but I have to say it would be a pretty chilling thing to watch as well!

Soon-to-be-disgraced Director of National Intelligence James Clapper and CIA Director John Brennan were among the quartet of jaded intel creeps sent to dump a friendly word or ten in Trump's ear. Accompanying them were NSA Director Michael Rogers, and more notoriously, Gollum-smirking FBI director James Comey!

The classified version of the aforementioned report from this month obviously had more detail than the public domain summary. The ODNI report (Office of the Director of National Intelligence) sounds a little bit too much like a psy-op tactic for comfort.

Of course, it may quite possibly have been a proper procedural move, in order to keep the President informed; but you do have to wonder what was going on here, at a deeper level… If anything?

Fortunately, future instalments of this book series are going to provide us with even more grounds for suspicion. Up to this point in the story, some might argue there is still room for a reasonable degree of skepticism about the critics of the Russiagate mainstream media narrative.

However, as we go further down the rabbit-hole, we're going to see some even more hideous marvels…

Sleep tight.

THE FINAL INDIGNITY…?

Oh and by the way, Confused Jim Comey 'just passing by, while he's in the area' stays behind to speak with Trump after the others have left. Whether this is a deliberately sinister 'breaking ranks' move on his part, or a 'purely coincidental' gesture of intimidation the Failing Four had plotted in advance, he tells Trump about the Steele dossier.

Well, we're going to have to leave Cryin' James Comey there to lick his wounds. Trump's refusal to bow to what may well strike many people reading today as little more than shallow intimidation tactics, leaves a bad taste in the mouth. But there's plenty more where that came from…

TO BE CONTINUED.

CONCLUSIONS?

So what conclusions can we draw from this sad and sorry tale?

Firstly, the mainstream media and the liberal elites have sorely underestimated the first true post-globalist US President. Secondly, they have very much underestimated the passion and the power of the American people to Make America Great Again!

The howls of derisive laughter that greeted Trump from the very first moment of his campaign have quickly been turned to tears: not the tears of innocence, but of thwarted rage and malice. The 'joke candidate' has truly had the last laugh, and Hillary 'Electability' Clinton has been sent packing. The very idea of her running again is laughable.

In the meantime, as the race for 2020 already heats up, our latest Captain Electability himself, Sleepy Joe Biden, has been dozing. Filling himself with grandiose delusions (how ironic!) of single-handedly saving America from itself, he has grossly misjudged the mood of the American people. While Trump had a poor showing in earlier polls, the previous campaign's numbers were so badly off-kilter as to threaten the basic credibility of polling as even an approximate science.

And as Trump continues to surge up and continually *improve* his polling, even the highly questionable polling strategies of the Alt-Left and Alt-Center make them look every bit as ludicrous and buffoonish of the Alt-Right of Richard Spencer and Andrew Anglin. The true alternative to all three alternatives, or 'Alts,' is patriotic populism, that both unifies *and* divides.

Trump's populism is in some ways 'divisive,' something of a dirty word; even though 'divisiveness' has been a key weapon against tyranny in America, ever since the days of the Revolution. To protest against injustice, fraud and servitude is *by definition* a divisive act; for as Barry Goldwater famously said, there is no extremism in the defense of liberty.

But Trump's populism, at the same time, is curiously unifying: and this is the bit you often *don't* get to hear in the mainstream media. Trump has done what once might have seemed impossible to many people, and has managed to unite people of all demographics around the *values* that made America Great, and that are already making her Great Again; rather than retreating into the shallow, barren trenches of either majoritarian or minoritarian 'identity politics...'

Or at least 'identity politics' as we know it: the kind of identity politics that places identity over values, instead of finding the shared values that are capable of cutting across all identities.

Is such a new identity politics possible? Well, there are certainly plenty of grassroots groups and concepts like Gays for Trump, LGBTrump, Blacks for Trump, Blexit, Walk Away and so many, many more!

How is it possible to reject identity politics, at least in the conventional sense, and yet to speak of all these specific demographics and movements?

The answer is simply this. The identity politics Trump is doing is very different from old school identity politics. There may well be a politics of identity here, but it is a politics that invites people of *all* demographics to work together on a truly *common* project: one of shared American and indeed human values, that places a consensus of civilized, noble and freedom loving values over the purely sectarian, petty and divisive politics of partisan identitarianism.

This doesn't mean, of course, that everyone in America shares the same interests. Conflicts of interests will always occur, for that is part of the nature not only of politics, but of human society itself.

The difference, however, is that by taking conflicts of interests seriously, rather than waving them away like Sanders with his 99% vs 1% rhetoric, or Clinton with her elitist technocratic 'managerial state,' Trump has helped open up America to proper democratic processes. And no amount of bad faith shrieks of 'racism,' 'misogyny,' or any other cynical accusation, will ever be able to take away Trump's achievement, nor that of all those who have helped him labor towards it; within and without the Beltway!

The old school, Darwinian, zero-sum, irredeemably narcissistic identity politics of the past has not healed the divisions of America; instead, it has manufactured mayhem! And every one of the gods of this world, from decrepit politicians to pompous intellectuals, from shady intel creeps to confused celebrities and slippery fake news gurus, knows this. The establishment know, beyond the merest shadow of a doubt, that a people once divided is easy to govern…

For a while.

As social consensus breaks down and all that is solid melts into air, people are at each other's throats, and the soft, sweet, winnowing tides of moral suasion give way to the iron jackboot of the law.

The ongoing breakdown of social solidarity and the incessant decay of once-shared values provide the perfect excuse for increasing the scope of government, and for normalizing coercive punishment, instead of drawing strength from the incredible values and traditions that we already have!

All this poses an existential threat to the United States of America; and in order to fight it, one has to fight fire with fire. The mainstream media often denounce Fox News as 'fake news,' and they are ferociously condemnatory towards Breitbart. However, part of the genius of the late, great, sorely, sorely lamented Andrew Breitbart, is precisely to take note of the Alinsky-like tactics of the radical left, and turn them back upon the perpetrators.

Just as the Children of Israel raided the treasures of Egypt in their exodus from servitude, tyranny and arbitrary power, and the early Christian Church took what they could from the surrounding society and turned it against them in the cause of freedom; so also have figures like Andrew Breitbart, Steve Bannon, John Nolte, Tucker Carlson and David Horowitz disarmed the 'Alt-Left,' as we call them nowadays, and turned their own weapons against them.

This is not so much an abandonment of reason and logic, as a rearmament of them. Reason and logic are always necessary, and cannot once be sacrificed; but in order to be fully effective, a little more is needed.

The most rational arguments in the world are to no avail if they cannot be made appealing. The old conflict between reason and rhetoric is largely illusory. There is simply no *essential* contradiction between the two.

Even if, in practice, the two often run into conflict, this is very much a question of the misuse of rhetoric from the liberal media, establishment politicians and other self-appointed 'experts' and 'intellectuals.'

Expertise ought to bring humility, and knowing the limits of one's knowledge is every bit as important as knowing what one does know.

Rhetoric on its own is mere foam and bluster; Reason alone is a mere timid ripple upon the shallowest shores of America's freedom project. By skillfully bridging the gap between these two supposed opposites, Trump has succeeded to a remarkable degree in renewing the project of liberty in America and indeed the world as a whole, rather than merely diminishing and enervating it.

The split in the liberal psyche between irrational, emotive screeching and dull, idle, technocratic intellectualism mirrors a divide in the heart of the American soul itself, that has been a sickness of ours so profound, so distressing and so debilitating and troubling, that one could be forgiven for wondering how much of a gap truly exists between the New World and the Ancien Regime of Europe.

However, the recent economic explosion and the concurrent 'boom' in the free marketplace of ideas is sending America roaring ahead of the Old Continent; and in turn, the Founding Fathers and their latter day successors are managing to tug and haul Europe herself out of her boggy quagmire of indifference and apathy.

The UK is freeing itself from the servitude of the European Union; meanwhile, other countries begin to demand more respect for their national sovereignty.

The old guard of France and Germany are widely held in contempt, the French President Macron is widely derided and perceived as an old school Parisian boy wonder with possible mommy issues, who has been savagely cracking down on protestors for months on end in a way that can only be compared to the Chinese Communist Party or some wide-eyed, paranoid, unhinged dictator from the Middle East.

The fake news is consistently blasphemed against 24/7; while countless people are increasingly shameless about hot-button issues like Islamic extremism, illegal immigration, terrorism, street crime, the SJW cult and the hideous plague of antisemitism and antizionism that is currently infesting the entire continent.

While the free peoples of Europe, and all free hearts across the globe, deserve full credit, it is impossible to deny that Trump's audacity in not merely thinking the unthinkable, but in daring to say the absolutely unsayable, has been tremendously influential in changing the status quo not only in the United States of America, but across the world as a whole.

From Mumbai to Manchester, from Jakarta to Genoa, establishment insiders are widely ridiculed, and their sacred cows battered day and daily.

Correctness savages political correctness, freedom mauls untrammeled choice, equal treatment launches a full frontal assault on equal outcomes, audacious truth-telling trumps fake news; and ultimately, credulity unwillingly cedes to a radical skepticism of status quo talking points, fake intel and government talking points, ramping up the ridicule and denunciation to a fever pitch that is but little short of downright *pyromaniacal* in character!

But this streaming, blazing torrent of 'creative destruction' in the free marketplace of ideas, is a *boom* leading not to a catastrophic *recession* in the cause of freedom, but rather to a *bust* on the greatest organized crime racket of them all: the endlessly giddy revolving door of mere politics as usual, business as usual; a fake, pathetic, mundane, mediocre and radically inauthentic parody of democracy in the guise of real freedom, equality and fraternity. And that is something that just cannot, under any circumstances, be tolerated!

So, as we proceed to further volumes of this book, we'll see more of the questionable behavior, more of the sinister talking points, and more of the unbridled rage and despair of the unaccountable elites, elected and unelected alike, as they slip deeper and further into the bitter midnight gloom of historical oblivion.

KEY FIGURES

Here are some of the most important people so far, whether pro or anti-Trump.

Donald J. Trump

The 45th President of the United States of America. How much more of an introduction do you need? ... Oh, and he's going to make America Great Again. In fact, he already has!

Hillary Clinton (Crooked Hillary)

Trump's supposed shoe-in nemesis for the 2016 election. Part of the notorious Clinton Dynasty double act, HRC and her husband, Bill Clinton, appears to many American citizens and observers globally to be one of the most scandal-plagued politicians of today; hence Trump's viral jibe, 'Crooked Hillary.'

Constantly dogged by career-long accusations of hypocrisy, double standards, insincerity, dishonesty and graft (including some epic punching-rightward blows from Bernie fans and Greens), Clinton lost the election and had to crawl off to lick her wounds. However, she now has a great opportunity to pull a Blair and do plenty of lucrative speeches!

CNN

Cable News Network, commonly characterized by Trump as 'fake news,' has been relentlessly hostile towards the President; even before he became President!

In recent times, plunging figures and mass lay-offs make one wonder how long this establishment liberal media organization can survive. As Fox News becomes even more popular over time, it may well be that the old school politically correct talking points of CNN are about to become a relic of history.

James Comey

Disgraced FBI director James Comey has been disparaged by both Democrats and Republicans alike for his handling of Emailgate. For some, Comey's role in the Russiagate moral panic has raised disturbing questions.

Lisa Page and Peter Strzok

Everybody loves their comedy double acts. But the unintentionally hilarious text messages exchanged by bumbling FBI agents Page and Strzok are not merely some Keystone Copts skit. On the contrary, they have very serious implications for American Democracy. Their sarcastic jokes about Trump and his voters are no longer a private matter, and in certain circles, they are both considered very much disgraced figures!

John Brennan

Former CIA director John Brennan was a key intel figure at the time of Russiagate. He is known as an ardent Never Trumper who has accused Trump of collusion many times.

Julian Assange

The flamboyantly controversial head of Wikileaks played an important role in the US election, exposing relevant information about Hillary Clinton. In recent times, after seeking refuge in the Ecuadorian Embassy, Assange faces possible extradition to Sweden (over rape allegations) and the USA (for various counts related to his hacking).

Mitch McConnell

A leading figure in the Republican old guard, Mitch McConnell is a veteran of the older, more neoconservative era of the Republican Party. But as the old Latin saying goes: 'the times change, and we also change with them.' Writing this in the summer of 2019, the Republican leadership have already been long supportive of Trump, as the Democratic Clown Car is already beginning to spin off the giddy rails of basic political and moral sanity!

Reince Priebus

Priebus was the chairman of the Republican National Committee from 2011 to 2017. He later served as White House Chief of Staff from January to July 2017.

Adrian Hawkins

In September 2015, this FBI special agent alerted the DNC about the alleged Russian hacking.

Barack Obama

The 44th President of the United States of America is a highly controversial figure; indeed, he is one of the most heavily disparaged national leaders since Richard Nixon.

His contentious healthcare reforms, often known as the eponymous 'Obamacare,' led to a great deal of heated debate. His views on gun control are also widely considered extreme, and he has been known to make bizarre gaffes; such as when notoriously compared ISIS to a Jayvee team, a comment reminiscent of old school neocon Republican George W. Bush's 'bring 'em on' comment about terrorist insurgents. Obama also referred to impoverished small town voters in the Midwest as 'bitter' and as 'clinging to guns or religion or antipathy to people who aren't like them or anti-immigrant sentiment or anti-trade sentiment as a way to explain their frustrations.'

Perhaps most seriously of all, he appeared to undermine the First Amendment and threaten religious freedom by saying 'The future must not belong to those who slander the prophet of Islam.'

Now I'm quite sure that if anyone had ever once *dared* to say, 'The future must not belong to those who insult Jesus, the Son of God,' or 'there is no future for those who insult the prophet Moses,' there would have been hell to pay! But that's liberal double standards for you...

All that said, it seems pretty certain that Obama's single most destructive action was his war against Gaddafi and his countrymen, which he claimed did not require congressional approval, and which ultimately led to the current migrant crisis in Europe; not to mention the deeply, deeply ironic reintroduction of slavery into Libya.

Obama has also drawn criticism for his serious deficit of experience prior to becoming President; his association with controversial figures like the fiery preacher Reverend Jeremiah Wright and Bill Ayers of the Weather Underground terrorist organization; and last but not least, his strikingly bombastic oratorical style, which often focuses heavily on his own greatness, and is crammed to the rafters with a sumptuous but ultimately unsatisfying feast high-flown, flamboyant flights of fancy; often without much in the way of real, concrete substance to back it up.

Or as his erstwhile nomination rival Clinton has famously said:

'You never hear the specifics!'

Christopher Steele

This former FBI agent is widely known for the Pissgate dossier, which attributed some sickening sexual behavior to Donald Trump, thereby cementing the notion that the President was somehow vulnerable to blackmail by the Russians, and in thrall to Putin.

Michael Cohen

Michael Cohen is a once-trusted Trump lawyer who later turned against him as the establishment dialed up the heat. Although he once had a fairly privileged position, it seems as though, when the storm and fury has finally died down, he's going to be little more than a passing footnote in history.

Democratic National Committee (DNC)

The DNC exists to organize the selection of, and also to co-ordinate support for, Democratic candidates in various elections. Every four years, they hold the Democratic National Convention, in order to anoint their next Presidential candidate. Allegations of a rigged candidature for the 2016 election continue to dog the DNC to this very day.

Republican National Committee (RNC)

The RNC is the Republican Party's equivalent of the DNC. And like the Democrats, it has a Republican National Convention. Despite considerable hostility towards Trump from various old school neoconservative candidates, he managed to get the nomination in the end.

The Dukes, Cozy Bear,Fancy Bear

All alleged hacking collectives, associated with various apparent server breaches that may have hindered Hillary Clinton's election campaign.

GU/GRU

According to liberal conspiracy theorists, Trump did not win the 2016 election; rather, it was won by the GU, sometimes referred to by its previous name, GRU.

It is also known in English (in full) as the Main Directorate of the General Staff of the Armed Forces of the Russian Federation. The GU reports directly to the military, rather than to the President of Russia. Did the GU really hack the Democratic Party's servers, and if so, did they do it on their own impetus or under Putin's instructions?

Either way, the Russiagate mainstream narrative is just generally dubious at best.

Wikileaks

Wikileaks, the world-renowned whistleblowing organization, was founded in 2016. On their tenth anniversary in 2016, they claimed to have published over 10 million documents and ten million words already. But at the time of writing, Assange is no longer the director of Wikileaks.

Since September 2018, Kristinn Hrafnsson has been its editor-in-chief.

IMPORTANT DOCUMENTS

SOURCE 1

https://www.dhs.gov/news/2016/10/07/joint-statement-department-homeland-security-and-office-director-national

Joint Statement from the Department Of Homeland Security and Office of the Director of National Intelligence on Election Security.

Release Date: October 7, 2016
For Immediate Release
DHS Press Office
Contact: 202-282-8010

The U.S. Intelligence Community (USIC) is confident that the Russian Government directed the recent compromises of e-mails from US persons and institutions, including from US political organizations. The recent disclosures of alleged hacked e-mails on sites like DCLeaks.com and WikiLeaks and by the Guccifer 2.0 online persona are consistent with the methods and motivations of Russian-directed efforts. These thefts and disclosures are intended to interfere with the US election process. Such activity is not new to Moscow—the Russians have used similar tactics and techniques across Europe and Eurasia, for example, to influence public opinion there. We believe, based on the scope and sensitivity of these efforts, that only Russia's senior-most officials could have authorized these activities.

Some states have also recently seen scanning and probing of their election-related systems, which in most cases originated from servers operated by a Russian company. However, we are not now in a position to attribute this activity to the Russian Government. The USIC and the Department of Homeland Security (DHS) assess that it would be extremely difficult for someone, including a nation-state actor, to alter actual ballot counts or election results by cyber attack or intrusion. This assessment is based on the decentralized nature of our election system in this country and the number of protections state and local election officials have in place. States ensure that voting machines are not connected to the Internet, and there are numerous checks and balances as well as extensive oversight at multiple levels built into our election process.

Nevertheless, DHS continues to urge state and local election officials to be vigilant and seek cybersecurity assistance from DHS. A number of states have already done so. DHS is providing several services to state and local election officials to assist in their cybersecurity. These services include cyber 'hygiene' scans of Internet-facing systems, risk and vulnerability assessments, information sharing about cyber incidents, and best practices for securing voter registration databases and addressing potential cyber threats. DHS has convened an Election Infrastructure Cybersecurity Working Group with experts across all levels of government to raise awareness of cybersecurity risks potentially affecting election infrastructure and the elections process. Secretary Johnson and DHS officials are working directly with the National Association of Secretaries of State to offer assistance, share information, and provide additional resources to state and local officials.

SOURCE 2

https://www.us-cert.gov/sites/default/files/publications/ JAR_16-20296A_GRIZZLY%20STEPPE-2016-1229.pdf

GRIZZLY STEPPE – Russian Malicious Cyber Activity

This Joint Analysis Report (JAR) is the result of analytic efforts between the Department of Homeland Security (DHS) and the Federal Bureau of Investigation (FBI). This document provides technical details regarding the tools and infrastructure used by the Russian civilian and military intelligence Services (RIS) to compromise and exploit networks and endpoints associated with the U.S. election, as well as a range of U.S. Government, political, and private sector entities. The U.S. Government is referring to this malicious cyber activity by RIS as GRIZZLY STEPPE. Previous JARs have not attributed malicious cyber activity to specific countries or threat actors. However, public attribution of these activities to RIS is supported by technical indicators from the U.S. Intelligence Community, DHS, FBI, the private sector, and other entities.

This determination expands upon the Joint Statement released October 7, 2016, from the Department of Homeland Security and the Director of National Intelligence on Election Security. This activity by RIS is part of an ongoing campaign of cyber-enabled operations directed at the U.S. government and its citizens. These

cyber operations have included spearphishing campaigns targeting government organizations, critical infrastructure entities,
think tanks, universities, political organizations, and corporations leading to the theft of information.

In foreign countries, RIS actors conducted damaging and/or disruptive cyber-attacks, including attacks on critical infrastructure networks. In some cases, RIS actors masqueraded as third
parties, hiding behind false online personas designed to cause the
victim to misattribute the source of the attack. This JAR provides
technical indicators related to many of these operations, recom-
mended mitigations, suggested actions to take in response to
the indicators provided, and information on how to report such
incidents to the U.S. Government. The U.S. Government confirms
that two different RIS actors participated in the intrusion into a
U.S. political party. The first actor group, known as Advanced Per-
sistent Threat (APT) 29, entered into the party's systems in summer 2015, while the second, known as APT28, entered in spring
2016.
Both groups have historically targeted government organizations, think tanks, universities, and corporations around the
world. APT29 has been observed crafting targeted spearphishing campaigns leveraging web links to a malicious dropper; once
executed, the code delivers Remote Access Tools (RATs) and
evades detection using a range of techniques. APT28 is known for
leveraging domains that closely mimic those of targeted organizations and tricking potential victims into entering legitimate
credentials.

APT28 actors relied heavily on shortened URLs in their spearphishing email campaigns. Once APT28 and APT29 have access
to victims, both groups exfiltrate and analyze information to
gain intelligence value. These groups use this information to
craft highly targeted spearphishing campaigns.

These actors set up operational infrastructure to obfuscate their source infrastructure, host domains and malware for targeting organizations, establish command and control nodes, and harvest credentials and other valuable information from their targets. In summer 2015, an APT29 spearphishing campaign directed emails containing a malicious link to over 1,000 recipients, including multiple U.S. Government victims. APT29 used legitimate domains, to include domains associated with U.S. organizations and educational institutions, to host malware and send spearphishing emails.

In the course of that campaign, APT29 successfully compromised a U.S. political party. At least one targeted individual activated links to malware hosted on operational infrastructure of opened attachments containing malware. APT29 delivered malware to the political party's systems, established persistence, escalated privileges, enumerated active directory accounts, and exfiltrated email from several accounts through encrypted connections back through operational infrastructure.

In spring 2016, APT28 compromised the same political party, again via targeted spearphishing. This time, the spearphishing email tricked recipients into changing their passwords through a fake webmail domain hosted on APT28 operational infrastructure.

Using the harvested credentials, APT28 was able to gain access and steal content, likely leading to the exfiltration of information from multiple senior party members. The U.S. Government assesses that information was leaked to the press and publicly disclosed.

Actors likely associated with RIS are continuing to engage in spearphishing campaigns, including one launched as recently as November 2016, just days after the U.S. election.

Technical Details

Indicators of Compromise (IOCs) IOCs associated with RIS cyber actors are provided within the accompanying .csv and .stix files of JAR-16-20296.

Yara Signature rule PAS_TOOL_PHP_WEB_KIT { meta: description = 'PAS TOOL PHP WEB KIT FOUND' strings: $php = '<? php' $base64decode = /\='base'\.\(\(\d+*\d+\)\.'_de'\.'code'/ $str-replace = '(str_replace(' $md5 = '.substr(md5(strrev(' $gzinflate = 'gzinflate' $cookie = '_COOKIE' $isset = 'isset' condition: (filesize > 20KB and filesize < 22KB) and #cookie == 2 and #isset == 3 and all of them }

Actions to Take Using Indicators

DHS recommends that network administrators review the IP addresses, file hashes, and Yara signature provided and add the IPs to their watchlist to determine whether malicious activity has been observed within their organizations. The review of network perimeter netflow or firewall logs will assist in determining whether your network has experienced suspicious activity.

When reviewing network perimeter logs for the IP addresses, organizations may find numerous instances of these IPs attempting to connect to their systems. Upon reviewing the traffic from these IPs, some traffic may correspond to malicious activity, and some may correspond to legitimate activity.

Some traffic that may appear legitimate is actually malicious, such as vulnerability scanning or browsing of legitimate public facing services (e.g., HTTP, HTTPS, FTP). Connections from these IPs may be performing vulnerability scans attempting to identify websites that are vulnerable to cross-site scripting (XSS) or Structured Query Language (SQL) injection attacks. If scanning identified vulnerable sites, attempts to exploit the vulnerabilities may be experienced.

Network administrators are encouraged to check their public-facing websites for the malicious file hashes. System owners are also advised to run the Yara signature on any system that is suspected to have been targeted by RIS actors.

Threats from IOCs Malicious actors may use a variety of methods to interfere with information systems. Some methods of attack are listed below. Guidance provided is applicable to many other computer networks.
• Injection Flaws are broad web application attack techniques that attempt to send commands to a browser, database, or other system, allowing a regular user to control behavior. The most common example is SQL injection, which subverts the relationship between a webpage and its supporting database, typically to obtain information contained inside the database. Another form is command injection, where an untrusted user is able to send commands to operating systems supporting a web application or database. See the United States Computer Emergency Readiness Team (US-CERT) Publication on SQL Injection for more information.

• Cross-site scripting (XSS) vulnerabilities allow threat actors to insert and execute unauthorized code in web applications. Successful XSS attacks on websites can provide the attacker unauthorized access. For prevention and mitigation strategies against XSS, see US-CERT's Alert on Compromised Web Servers and Web Shells.

• Server vulnerabilities may be exploited to allow unauthorized access to sensitive information. An attack against a poorly configured server may allow an adversary access to critical information including any websites or databases hosted on the server. See US-CERT's Tip on Website Security for additional information.

Recommended Mitigations
Commit to Cybersecurity Best Practices

A commitment to good cybersecurity and best practices is critical to protecting networks and systems. Here are some questions you may want to ask your organization to help prevent and mitigate against attacks.

Backups: Do we backup all critical information? Are the backups stored offline? Have we tested our ability to revert to backups during an incident?

1. Risk Analysis: Have we conducted a cybersecurity risk analysis of the organization?
2. Staff Training: Have we trained staff on cybersecurity best practices?
3. Vulnerability Scanning & Patching: Have we implemented regular scans of our network and systems and appropriate patching of known system vulnerabilities?
4. Application Whitelisting: Do we allow only approved programs to run on our networks?
5. Incident Response: Do we have an incident response plan and have we practiced it?
6. Business Continuity: Are we able to sustain business operations without access to certain systems? For how long? Have we tested this?
7. Penetration Testing: Have we attempted to hack into our own systems to test the security of our systems and our ability to defend against attacks?

Top Seven Mitigation Strategies

DHS encourages network administrators to implement the recommendations below, which can prevent as many as 85 percent of targeted cyber-attacks. These strategies are common sense to many, but DHS continues to see intrusions because organizations fail to use these basic measures.Patch applications and operating systems – Vulnerable applications and operating systems are the targets of most attacks. Ensuring these are patched with the latest updates greatly reduces the number of exploitable entry points available to an attacker.

Use best practices when updating software and patches by only downloading updates from authenticated vendor sites. Application whitelisting – Whitelisting is one of the best security strategies because it allows only specified programs to run while blocking all others, including malicious software.

Restrict administrative privileges – Threat actors are increasingly focused on gaining control of legitimate credentials, especially those associated with highly privileged accounts.

Reduce privileges to only those needed for a user's duties. Separate administrators into privilege tiers with limited access to other tiers. Network Segmentation and Segregation into Security Zones – Segment networks into logical enclaves and restrict host-to-host communications paths. This helps protect sensitive information and critical services and limits damage from network perimeter breaches.

Input validation – Input validation is a method of sanitizing untrusted user input provided by users of a web application, and may prevent many types of web application security flaws, such as SQLi, XSS, and command injection. File Reputation – Tune Anti-Virus file reputation systems to the most aggressive setting possible; some products can limit execution to only the highest reputation files, stopping a wide range of untrustworthy code from gaining control.

Understanding firewalls – When anyone or anything can access your network at any time, your network is more susceptible to being attacked. Firewalls can be configured to block data from certain locations (IP whitelisting) or applications while allowing relevant and necessary data through.

1. Patch applications and operating systems – Vulnerable applications and operating systems are the targets of most attacks. Ensuring these are patched with the latest updates greatly reduces the number of exploitable entry points available to an attacker. Use best practices when updating software and patches by only downloading updates from authenticated vendor sites.
2. Application whitelisting – Whitelisting is one of the best security strategies because it allows only specified programs to run while blocking all others, including malicious software.
3. Restrict administrative privileges – Threat actors are increasingly focused on gaining control of legitimate credentials, especially those associated with highly privileged accounts. Reduce privileges to only those needed for a user's duties. Separate administrators into privilege tiers with limited access to other tiers.
4. Network Segmentation and Segregation into Security Zones – Segment networks into logical enclaves and restrict host-to-host communications paths. This helps protect sensitive information and critical services and limits damage from network perimeter breaches.
5. Input validation – Input validation is a method of sanitizing untrusted user input provided by users of a web application, and may prevent many types of web application security flaws, such as SQLi, XSS, and command injection.
6. File Reputation – Tune Anti-Virus file reputation systems to the most aggressive setting possible; some prod-

ucts can limit execution to only the highest reputation files, stopping a wide range of untrustworthy code from gaining control.

7. Understanding firewalls – When anyone or anything can access your network at any time, your network is more susceptible to being attacked. Firewalls can be configured to block data from certain locations (IP whitelisting) or applications while allowing relevant and necessary data through.

Responding to Unauthorized Access to Networks

Implement your security incident response and business continuity plan. It may take time for your organization's IT professionals to isolate and remove threats to your systems and restore normal operations. Meanwhile, you should take steps to maintain your organization's essential functions according to your business continuity plan. Organizations should maintain and regularly test backup plans, disaster recovery plans, and business continuity procedures.

Contact DHS or law enforcement immediately. We encourage you to contact DHS NCCIC (NCCICCustomerService@hq.dhs.gov or 888-282-0870), the FBI through a local field office or the FBI's Cyber Division (CyWatch@ic.fbi.gov or 855-292-3937) to report an intrusion and to request incident response resources or technical assistance.

Detailed Mitigation Strategies Protect

Protect Against SQL Injection and Other Attacks on Web Services

Routinely evaluate known and published vulnerabilities, perform software updates and technology refreshes periodically, and audit external-facing systems for known Web application vulnerabilities. Take steps to harden both Web applications and the servers hosting them to reduce the risk of network intrusion via this vector.

• Use and configure available firewalls to block attacks.

• Take steps to further secure Windows systems such as installing and configuring Microsoft's Enhanced Mitigation Experience Toolkit (EMET) and Microsoft AppLocker.

• Monitor and remove any unauthorized code present in any www directories.

• Disable, discontinue, or disallow the use of Internet Control Message Protocol (ICMP) and Simple Network Management Protocol (SNMP) and response to these protocols as much as possible.

• Remove non-required HTTP verbs from Web servers as typical Web servers and applications only require GET, POST, and HEAD.

• Where possible, minimize server fingerprinting by configuring Web servers to avoid responding with banners identifying the server software and version number.

• Secure both the operating system and the application.

• Update and patch production servers regularly.

• Disable potentially harmful SQL-stored procedure calls.

• Sanitize and validate input to ensure that it is properly typed and does not contain escaped code.

• Consider using type-safe stored procedures and prepared statements.

• Perform regular audits of transaction logs for suspicious activity.

• Perform penetration testing against Web services.

• Ensure error messages are generic and do not expose too much information.

Phishing and Spearphishing

• Implement a Sender Policy Framework (SPF) record for your organization's Domain Name System (DNS) zone file to minimize risks relating to the receipt of spoofed messages.

• Educate users to be suspicious of unsolicited phone calls, social media interactions, or email messages from individuals asking about employees or other internal information. If an unknown individual claims to be from a legitimate organization, try to verify his or her identity directly with the company.

• Do not provide personal information or information about your organization, including its structure or networks, unless you are certain of a person's authority to have the information.

• Do not reveal personal or financial information in social media or email, and do not respond to solicitations for this information. This includes following links sent in email.

• Pay attention to the URL of a website. Malicious websites may look identical to a legitimate site, but the URL often includes a variation in spelling or a different domain than the valid website (e.g., .com vs. .net).

• If you are unsure whether an email request is legitimate, try to verify it by contacting the company directly. Do not use contact information provided on a website connected to the request; instead, check previous statements for contact information. Information about known phishing attacks is also available online from groups such as the Anti-Phishing Working Group (http://www.antiphishing.org).

• Take advantage of anti-phishing features offered by your email client and web browser.

• Patch all systems for critical vulnerabilities, prioritizing timely patching of software that processes Internet data, such as web browsers, browser plugins, and document readers.

Permissions, Privileges, and Access Controls

• Reduce privileges to only those needed for a user's duties.

• Restrict users' ability (permissions) to install and run unwanted software applications, and apply the principle of 'Least Privilege' to all systems and services. Restricting these privileges may prevent malware from running or limit its capability to spread through the network.

• Carefully consider the risks before granting administrative rights to users on their own machines.

• Scrub and verify all administrator accounts regularly.

• Configure Group Policy to restrict all users to only one login session, where possible.

• Enforce secure network authentication where possible.

• Instruct administrators to use non-privileged accounts for standard functions such as Web browsing or checking Web mail. Segment networks into logical enclaves and restrict host-to-host communication paths. Containment provided by enclaving also makes incident cleanup significantly less costly.

• Configure firewalls to disallow RDP traffic coming from outside of the network boundary, except for in specific configurations such as when tunneled through a secondary VPN with lower privileges.

• Audit existing firewall rules and close all ports that are not explicitly needed for business. Specifically, carefully consider which ports should be connecting outbound versus inbound.

• Enforce a strict lockout policy for network users and closely monitor logs for failed login activity. This can be indicative of failed intrusion activity.

• If remote access between zones is an unavoidable business need, log and monitor these connections closely.

• In environments with a high risk of interception or intrusion, organizations should consider supplementing password authentication with other forms of authentication such as challenge/response or multifactor authentication using biometric or physical tokens.

Credentials

• Enforce a tiered administrative model with dedicated administrator workstations and separate administrative accounts that are used exclusively for each tier to prevent tools, such as Mimikatz, for credential theft from harvesting domain-level credentials.

• Implement multi-factor authentication (e.g., smart cards) or at minimum ensure users choose complex passwords that change regularly.

• Be aware that some services (e.g., FTP, telnet, and .rlogin) transmit user credentials in clear text. Minimize the use of these services where possible or consider more secure alternatives.

• Properly secure password files by making hashed passwords more difficult to acquire. Password hashes can be cracked within seconds using freely available tools. Consider restricting access to sensitive password hashes by using a shadow password file or equivalent on UNIX systems.

• Replace or modify services so that all user credentials are passed through an encrypted channel.

• Avoid password policies that reduce the overall strength of credentials. Policies to avoid include lack of password expiration date, lack of lockout policy, low or disabled password complexity requirements, and password history set to zero.

• Ensure that users are not re-using passwords between zones by setting policies and conducting regular audits.

• Use unique passwords for local accounts for each device.

Logging Practices

• Ensure event logging (applications, events, login activities, security attributes, etc.) is turned on or monitored for identification of security issues.

• Configure network logs to provide enough information to assist in quickly developing an accurate determination of a security incident.

• Upgrade PowerShell to new versions with enhanced logging features and monitor the logs to detect usage of PowerShell commands, which are often malware-related.

• Secure logs, potentially in a centralized location, and protect them from modification.

• Prepare an incident response plan that can be rapidly implemented in case of a cyber intrusion.

How to Enhance Your Organization's Cybersecurity Posture

DHS offers a variety of resources for organizations to help recognize and address their cybersecurity risks. Resources include discussion points, steps to start evaluating a cybersecurity program, and a list of hands-on resources available to organizations. For a list of services, visit https://www.us-cert.gov/ccubedvp. Other resources include:

• The Cyber Security Advisors (CSA) program bolsters cybersecurity preparedness, risk mitigation, and incident response capabilities of critical infrastructure entities and more closely aligns them with the Federal Government. CSAs are DHS personnel assigned to districts throughout the country and territories, with at least one advisor in each of the 10 CSA regions, which mirror the Federal Emergency Management Agency regions. For more information, email cyberadvisor@hq.dhs.gov.

• Cyber Resilience Review (CRR) is a no-cost, voluntary assessment to evaluate and enhance cybersecurity within critical infrastructure sectors, as well as state, local, tribal, and territorial governments. The goal of the CRR is to develop an understanding and measurement of key cybersecurity capabilities to provide meaningful indicators of an entity's operational resilience and ability to manage cyber risk to critical services during normal operations and times of operational stress and crisis. Visit https://www.cert.org/resilience/rmm.html to learn more about the CERT Resilience Management Model.

• Enhanced Cybersecurity Services (ECS) helps critical infrastructure owners and operators protect their systems by sharing sensitive and classified cyber threat information with Commercial Service Providers (CSPs) and Operational Implementers (OIs). CSPs then use the cyber threat information to protect CI customers. OIs use the threat information to protect internal networks. For more information, email ECS_Program@hq.dhs.gov.

• The Cybersecurity Information Sharing and Collaboration Program (CISCP) is a voluntary information-sharing and collaboration program between and among critical infrastructure partners and the Federal Government. For more information, email CISCP@us-cert.gov.

• The Automated Indicator Sharing (AIS) initiative is a DHS effort to create a system where as soon as a company or federal agency observes an attempted compromise, the indicator will be shared in real time with all of our partners, protecting them from that particular threat. That means adversaries can only use an attack once, which increases their costs and ultimately reduces the prevalence of cyber-attacks. While AIS will not eliminate sophisticated cyber threats, it will allow companies and federal agencies to concentrate more on them by clearing away less sophisticated attacks.

AIS participants connect to a DHS-managed system in the NCCIC that allows bidirectional sharing of cyber threat indicators. A server housed at each participant's location allows each to exchange indicators with the NCCIC. Participants will not only receive DHS-developed indicators, but can share indicators they have observed in their own network defense efforts, which DHS will then share with all AIS participants. For more information, visit https://www.dhs.gov/ais.

• The Cybersecurity Framework (Framework), developed by the National Institute of Standards and Technology (NIST) in collaboration with the public and private sectors, is a tool that can improve the cybersecurity readiness of entities.

The Framework enables entities, regardless of size, degree of cyber risk, or cyber sophistication, to apply principles and best practices of risk management to improve the security and resiliency of critical infrastructure. The Framework provides standards, guidelines, and practices that are working effectively today. It consists of three parts—the Framework Core, the Framework Profile, and Framework Implementation Tiers—and emphasizes five functions: Identify, Protect, Detect, Respond, and Recover. Use of the Framework is strictly voluntary. For more information, visit https://www.nist.gov/cyberframework or email cyberframework@nist.gov.

Contact Information

Recipients of this report are encouraged to contribute any additional information that they may have related to this threat. Include the JAR reference number (JAR-16-20296A) in the subject line of all email correspondence.

For any questions related to this report, please contact NCCIC or the FBI.
NCCIC: Phone: +1-888-282-0870
Email: NCCICCustomerService@hq.dhs.gov
FBI: Phone: +1-855-292-3937
Email: cywatch@ic.fbi.gov

Feedback

NCCIC continuously strives to improve its products and services. You can help by answering a few short questions about this product at the following URL: https://www.us-cert.gov/forms/feedback.

SOURCE 3

https://www.dni.gov/files/documents/ICA_2017_01.pdf

*Background to 'Assessing Russian
Activities and Intentions in Recent
US Elections': The Analytic Process
and Cyber Incident Attribution*

*This report is a declassified version of a highly classified assessment;
its conclusions are identical to those in the highly classified
assessment but this version does not include the full supporting
information on key elements of the influence campaign.*

Background to 'Assessing Russian Activities and Intentions in Recent US Elections': The Analytic Process and Cyber Incident Attribution 'Assessing Russian Activities and Intentions in Recent US Elections' is a declassified version of a highly classified assessment that has been provided to the President and to recipients approved by the President.

• The Intelligence Community rarely can publicly reveal the full extent of its knowledge or the precise bases for its assessments, as the release of such information would reveal sensitive sources or methods and imperil the ability to collect critical foreign intelligence in the future.

• Thus, while the conclusions in the report are all reflected in the classified assessment, the declassified report does not and cannot include the full supporting information, including specific intelligence and sources and methods.

The Analytic Process

The mission of the Intelligence Community is to seek to reduce the uncertainty surrounding foreign activities, capabilities, or leaders' intentions. This objective is difficult to achieve when seeking to understand complex issues on which foreign actors go to extraordinary lengths to hide or obfuscate their activities.

• On these issues of great importance to US national security, the goal of intelligence analysis is to provide assessments to decisionmakers that are intellectually rigorous, objective, timely, and useful, and that adhere to tradecraft standards.

• The tradecraft standards for analytic products have been refined over the past ten years. These standards include describing sources (including their reliability and access to the information they provide), clearly expressing uncertainty, distinguishing between underlying information and analysts' judgments and assumptions, exploring alternatives, demonstrating relevance to the customer, using strong and transparent logic, and explaining change or consistency in judgments over time.

• Applying these standards helps ensure that the Intelligence Community provides US policymakers, warfighters, and operators with the best and most accurate insight, warning, and context, as well as potential opportunities to advance US national security.

Intelligence Community analysts integrate information from a wide range of sources, including human sources, technical collection, and open source information, and apply specialized skills and structured analytic tools to draw inferences informed by the data available, relevant past activity, and logic and reasoning to provide insight into what is happening and the prospects for the future.

• A critical part of the analyst's task is to explain uncertainties associated with major judgments based on the quantity and quality of the source material, information gaps, and the complexity of the issue.

• When Intelligence Community analysts use words such as 'we assess' or 'we judge,' they are conveying an analytic assessment or judgment.

• Some analytic judgments are based directly on collected information; others rest on previous judgments, which serve as building blocks in rigorous analysis. In either type of judgment, the tradecraft standards outlined above ensure that analysts have an appropriate basis for the judgment.

• Intelligence Community judgments often include two important elements: judgments of how likely it is that something has happened or will happen (using terms such as 'likely' or 'unlikely') and confidence levels in those judgments (low, moderate, and high) that refer to the evidentiary basis, logic and reasoning, and precedents that underpin the judgments.

Determining Attribution in
Cyber Incidents

The nature of cyberspace makes attribution of cyber operations difficult but not impossible. Every kind of cyber operation—malicious or not—leaves a trail. US Intelligence Community analysts use this information, their constantly growing knowledge base of previous events and known malicious actors, and their knowledge of how these malicious actors work and the tools that they use, to attempt to trace these operations back to their source. In every case, they apply the same tradecraft standards described in the Analytic Process above.

• Analysts consider a series of questions to assess how the information compares with existing knowledge and adjust their confidence in their judgments as appropriate to account for any alternative hypotheses and ambiguities.

• An assessment of attribution usually is not a simple statement of who conducted an operation, but rather a series of judgments that describe whether it was an isolated incident, who was the likely perpetrator, that perpetrator's possible motivations, and whether a foreign government had a role in ordering or leading the operation.

Scope and Sourcing

Information available as of 29 December 2016 was used in the preparation of this product.

Scope

This report includes an analytic assessment drafted and coordinated among The Central Intelligence Agency (CIA), The Federal Bureau of Investigation (FBI), and The National Security Agency (NSA), which draws on intelligence information collected and disseminated by those three agencies. It covers the motivation and scope of Moscow's intentions regarding US elections and Moscow's use of cyber tools and media campaigns to influence US public opinion.

The assessment focuses on activities aimed at the 2016 US presidential election and draws on our understanding of previous Russian influence operations. When we use the term 'we' it refers to an assessment by all three agencies.

• This report is a declassified version of a highly classified assessment. This document's conclusions are identical to the highly classified assessment, but this document does not include the full supporting information, including specific intelligence on key elements of the influence campaign. Given the redactions, we made minor edits purely for readability and flow.

We did not make an assessment of the impact that Russian activities had on the outcome of the 2016 election. The US Intelligence Community is charged with monitoring and assessing the intentions, capabilities, and actions of foreign actors; it does not analyze US political processes or US public opinion.

• New information continues to emerge, providing increased insight into Russian activities.

Sourcing

Many of the key judgments in this assessment rely on a body of reporting from multiple sources that are consistent with our understanding of Russian behavior. Insights into Russian efforts —including specific cyber operations—and Russian views of key US players derive from multiple corroborating sources.

Some of our judgments about Kremlin preferences and intent are drawn from the behavior of Kremlin loyal political figures, state media, and pro-Kremlin social media actors, all of whom the Kremlin either directly uses to convey messages or who are answerable to the Kremlin.

The Russian leadership invests significant resources in both foreign and domestic propaganda and places a premium on transmitting what it views as consistent, self-reinforcing narratives regarding its desires and redlines, whether on Ukraine, Syria, or relations with the United States.

Key Judgments

Russian efforts to influence the 2016 US presidential election represent the most recent expression of Moscow's longstanding desire to undermine the US-led liberal democratic order, but these activities demonstrated a significant escalation in directness, level of activity, and scope of effort compared to previous operations.

We assess Russian President Vladimir Putin ordered an influence campaign in 2016 aimed at the US presidential election. Russia's goals were to undermine public faith in the US democratic process, denigrate Secretary Clinton, and harm her electability and potential presidency. We further assess Putin and the Russian Government developed a clear preference for President-elect Trump. We have high confidence in these judgments.

• We also assess Putin and the Russian Government aspired to help President-elect Trump's election chances when possible by discrediting Secretary Clinton and publicly contrasting her unfavorably to him. All three agencies agree with this judgment. CIA and FBI have high confidence in this judgment; NSA has moderate confidence.

• Moscow's approach evolved over the course of the campaign based on Russia's understanding of the electoral prospects of the two main candidates. When it appeared to Moscow that Secretary Clinton was likely to win the election, the Russian influence campaign began to focus more on undermining her future presidency.

• Further information has come to light since Election Day that, when combined with Russian behavior since early November 2016, increases our confidence in our assessments of Russian motivations and goals.

Moscow's influence campaign followed a Russian messaging strategy that blends covert intelligence operations—such as cyber activity—with overt efforts by Russian Government agencies, state-funded media, third-party intermediaries, and paid social media users or 'trolls.' Russia, like its Soviet predecessor, has a history of conducting covert influence campaigns focused on US presidential elections that have used intelligence officers and agents and press placements to disparage candidates perceived as hostile to the Kremlin.

• Russia's intelligence services conducted cyber operations against targets associated with the 2016 US presidential election, including targets associated with both major US political parties.

• We assess with high confidence that Russian military intelligence (General Staff Main Intelligence Directorate or GRU) used the Guccifer 2.0 persona and DCLeaks.com to release US victim data obtained in cyber operations publicly and in exclusives to media outlets and relayed material to WikiLeaks.

• Russian intelligence obtained and maintained access to elements of multiple US state or local electoral boards. DHS assesses that the types of systems Russian actors targeted or compromised were not involved in vote tallying.

• Russia's state-run propaganda machine contributed to the influence campaign by serving as a platform for Kremlin messaging to

Russian and international audiences.

We assess Moscow will apply lessons learned from its Putin-ordered campaign aimed at the US presidential election to future influence efforts worldwide, including against US allies and their election processes.

Russia's Influence Campaign Targeting the 2016 US Presidential Election

Putin Ordered Campaign To Influence US Election

We assess with high confidence that Russian President Vladimir Putin ordered an influence campaign in 2016 aimed at the US presidential election, the consistent goals of which were to undermine public faith in the US democratic process, denigrate Secretary Clinton, and harm her electability and potential presidency.

We further assess Putin and the Russian Government developed a clear preference for President-elect Trump. When it appeared to Moscow that Secretary Clinton was likely to win the election, the Russian influence campaign then focused on undermining her expected presidency.

• We also assess Putin and the Russian Government aspired to help President-elect Trump's election chances when possible by discrediting Secretary Clinton and publicly contrasting her unfavorably to him. All three agencies agree with this judgment. CIA and FBI have high confidence in this judgment; NSA has moderate confidence.

• In trying to influence the US election, we assess the Kremlin sought to advance its longstanding desire to undermine the US-led liberal democratic order, the promotion of which Putin and other senior Russian leaders view as a threat to Russia and Putin's regime.

• Putin publicly pointed to the Panama Papers disclosure and the Olympic doping scandal as US-directed efforts to defame Russia, suggesting he sought to use disclosures to discredit the image of the United States and cast it as hypocritical.

• Putin most likely wanted to discredit Secretary Clinton because he has publicly blamed her since 2011 for inciting mass protests against his regime in late 2011 and early 2012, and because he holds a grudge for comments he almost certainly saw as disparaging him.

We assess Putin, his advisers, and the Russian Government developed a clear preference for President-elect Trump over Secretary Clinton.

• Beginning in June, Putin's public comments about the US presidential race avoided directly praising President-elect Trump, probably because Kremlin officials thought that any praise from Putin personally would backfire in the United States. Nonetheless, Putin publicly indicated a preference for President-elect Trump's stated policy to work with Russia, and pro-Kremlin figures spoke highly about what they saw as his Russia-friendly positions on Syria and Ukraine. Putin publicly contrasted the President-elect's approach to Russia with Secretary Clinton's 'aggressive rhetoric.'

• Moscow also saw the election of President elect Trump as a way to achieve an international counterterrorism coalition against the Islamic State in Iraq and the Levant (ISIL).

• Putin has had many positive experiences working with Western political leaders whose business interests made them more disposed to deal with Russia, such as former Italian Prime Minister Silvio Berlusconi and former German Chancellor Gerhard Schroeder.

• Putin, Russian officials, and other pro-Kremlin pundits stopped publicly criticizing the US election process as unfair almost immediately after the election because Moscow probably assessed it would be counterproductive to building positive relations.

We assess the influence campaign aspired to help President-elect Trump's chances of victory when possible by discrediting Secretary Clinton and publicly contrasting her unfavorably to the President-elect.

When it appeared to Moscow that Secretary Clinton was likely to win the presidency the Russian influence campaign focused more on undercutting Secretary Clinton's legitimacy and crippling her presidency from its start, including by impugning the fairness of the election.

• Before the election, Russian diplomats had publicly denounced the US electoral process and were prepared to publicly call into question the validity of the results. Pro Kremlin bloggers had prepared a Twitter campaign, #DemocracyRIP, on election night in anticipation of Secretary Clinton's victory, judging from their social media activity.

Russian Campaign Was Multifaceted

Moscow's use of disclosures during the US election was unprecedented, but its influence campaign otherwise followed a longstanding Russian messaging strategy that blends covert intelligence operations—such as cyber activity—with overt efforts by Russian Government agencies, statefunded media, third-party intermediaries, and paid social media users or 'trolls.'

• We assess that influence campaigns are approved at the highest levels of the Russian Government—particularly those that would be politically sensitive.

• Moscow's campaign aimed at the US election reflected years of investment in its capabilities, which Moscow has honed in the former Soviet states.

• By their nature, Russian influence campaigns are multifaceted and designed to be deniable because they use a mix of agents of influence, cutouts, front organizations, and false-flag operations. Moscow demonstrated this during the Ukraine crisis in 2014, when Russia deployed forces and advisers to eastern Ukraine and denied it publicly.

The Kremlin's campaign aimed at the US election featured disclosures of data obtained through Russian cyber operations; intrusions into US state and local electoral boards; and overt propaganda. Russian intelligence collection both informed and enabled the influence campaign.

Cyber Espionage Against US Political Organizations

Russia's intelligence services conducted cyber operations against targets associated with the 2016 US presidential election, including targets associated with both major US political parties.

We assess Russian intelligence services collected against the US primary campaigns, think tanks, and lobbying groups they viewed as likely to shape future US policies. In July 2015, Russian intelligence gained access to Democratic National Committee (DNC) networks and maintained that access until at least June 2016.

• The General Staff Main Intelligence Directorate (GRU) probably began cyber operations aimed at the US election by March 2016. We assess that the GRU operations resulted in the compromise of the personal e-mail accounts of Democratic Party officials and political figures. By May, the GRU had exfiltrated large volumes of data from the DNC.

Public Disclosures of Russian-Collected Data

We assess with high confidence that the GRU used the Guccifer 2.0 persona, DCLeaks.com, and WikiLeaks to release US victim data obtained in cyber operations publicly and in exclusives to media outlets.

• Guccifer 2.0, who claimed to be an independent Romanian hacker, made multiple contradictory statements and false claims about his likely Russian identity throughout the election. Press reporting suggests more than one person claiming to be Guccifer 2.0 interacted with journalists.

• Content that we assess was taken from e-mail accounts targeted by the GRU in March 2016 appeared on DCLeaks.com starting in June.

We assess with high confidence that the GRU relayed material it acquired from the DNC and senior Democratic officials to WikiLeaks. Moscow most likely chose WikiLeaks because of its self-proclaimed reputation for authenticity. Disclosures through WikiLeaks did not contain any evident forgeries.

• In early September, Putin said publicly it was important the DNC data was exposed to WikiLeaks, calling the search for the source of the leaks a distraction and denying Russian 'state-level' involvement.

• The Kremlin's principal international propaganda outlet RT (formerly Russia Today) has actively collaborated with Wiki-Leaks. RT's editor-in-chief visited WikiLeaks founder Julian Assange at the Ecuadorian Embassy in London in August 2013, where they discussed renewing his broadcast contract with RT, according to Russian and Western media. Russian media subsequently announced that RT had become 'the only Russian media company' to partner with WikiLeaks and had received access to 'new leaks of secret information.' RT routinely gives Assange sympathetic coverage and provides him a platform to denounce the United States.

These election-related disclosures reflect a pattern of Russian intelligence using hacked information in targeted influence efforts against targets such as Olympic athletes and other foreign governments. Such efforts have included releasing or altering personal data, defacing websites, or releasing emails.

• A prominent target since the 2016 Summer Olympics has been the World Anti-Doping Agency (WADA), with leaks that we assess to have originated with the GRU and that have involved data on US athletes.

Russia collected on some Republican-affiliated targets but did not conduct a comparable disclosure campaign.

Russian Cyber Intrusions Into State and Local Electoral Boards.

Russian intelligence accessed elements of multiple state or local electoral boards. Since early 2014, Russian intelligence has researched US electoral processes and related technology and equipment.

• DHS assesses that the types of systems we observed Russian actors targeting or compromising are not involved in vote tallying.

Russian Propaganda Efforts.

Russia's state-run propaganda machine—comprised of its domestic media apparatus, outlets targeting global audiences such as RT and Sputnik, and a network of quasi-government trolls—contributed to the influence campaign by serving as a platform for Kremlin messaging to Russian and international audiences. State-owned Russian media made increasingly favorable comments about President elect Trump as the 2016 US general and primary election campaigns progressed while consistently offering negative coverage of Secretary Clinton.

• Starting in March 2016, Russian Government– linked actors began openly supporting President-elect Trump's candidacy in media aimed at English-speaking audiences. RT and Sputnik—another government-funded outlet producing pro-Kremlin radio and online content in a variety of languages for international audiences—consistently cast President-elect Trump as the target of unfair coverage from traditional US media outlets that they claimed were subservient to a corrupt political establishment.

• Russian media hailed President-elect Trump's victory as a vindication of Putin's advocacy of global populist movements—the theme of Putin's annual conference for Western academics in October 2016—and the latest example of Western liberalism's collapse.

• Putin's chief propagandist Dmitriy Kiselev used his flagship weekly newsmagazine program this fall to cast President-elect Trump as an outsider victimized by a corrupt political establishment and faulty democratic election process that aimed to prevent his election because of his desire to work with Moscow.

• Pro-Kremlin proxy Vladimir Zhirinovskiy, leader of the nationalist Liberal Democratic Party of Russia, proclaimed just before the election that if President-elect Trump won, Russia would 'drink champagne' in anticipation of being able to advance its positions on Syria and Ukraine.

RT's coverage of Secretary Clinton throughout the US presidential campaign was consistently negative and focused on her leaked e-mails and accused her of corruption, poor physical and mental health, and ties to Islamic extremism. Some Russian officials echoed Russian lines for the influence campaign that Secretary Clinton's election could lead to a war between the United States and Russia.

• In August, Kremlin-linked political analysts suggested avenging negative Western reports on Putin by airing segments devoted to Secretary Clinton's alleged health problems.

• On 6 August, RT published an English language video called 'Julian Assange Special: Do WikiLeaks Have the E-mail That'll Put Clinton in Prison?' and an exclusive interview with Assange entitled 'Clinton and ISIS Funded by the Same Money.' RT's most popular video on Secretary Clinton, 'How 100% of the Clintons' 'Charity' Went to…Themselves,' had more than 9 million views on social media platforms. RT's most popular English language video about the President-elect, called 'Trump Will Not Be Permitted To Win,' featured Assange and had 2.2 million views.

• For more on Russia's past media efforts— including portraying the 2012 US electoral process as undemocratic—please see Annex A: Russia—Kremlin's TV Seeks To Influence Politics, Fuel Discontent in US.

Russia used trolls as well as RT as part of its influence efforts to denigrate Secretary Clinton. This effort amplified stories on scandals about Secretary Clinton and the role of WikiLeaks in the election campaign.

• The likely financier of the so-called Internet Research Agency of professional trolls located in Saint Petersburg is a close Putin ally with ties to Russian intelligence.

• A journalist who is a leading expert on the Internet Research Agency claimed that some social media accounts that appear to be tied to Russia's professional trolls—because they previously were devoted to supporting Russian actions in Ukraine—started to advocate for President-elect Trump as early as December 2015.

Influence Effort Was Boldest Yet in the US

Russia's effort to influence the 2016 US presidential election represented a significant escalation in directness, level of activity, and scope of effort compared to previous operations aimed at US elections.

We assess the 2016 influence campaign reflected the Kremlin's recognition of the worldwide effects that mass disclosures of US Government and other private data—such as those conducted by WikiLeaks and others—have achieved in recent years, and their understanding of the value of orchestrating such disclosures to maximize the impact of compromising information.

• During the Cold War, the Soviet Union used intelligence officers, influence agents, forgeries, and press placements to disparage candidates perceived as hostile to the Kremlin, according to a former KGB archivist.

Since the Cold War, Russian intelligence efforts related to US elections have primarily focused on foreign intelligence collection. For decades, Russian and Soviet intelligence services have sought to collect insider information from US political parties that could help Russian leaders understand a new US administration's plans and priorities.

• The Russian Foreign Intelligence Service (SVR) Directorate S (Illegals) officers arrested in the United States in 2010 reported to Moscow about the 2008 election.

• In the 1970s, the KGB recruited a Democratic Party activist who reported information about then-presidential hopeful Jimmy Carter's campaign and foreign policy plans, according to a former KGB archivist.

Election Operation Signals 'New Normal' in Russian Influence Efforts

We assess Moscow will apply lessons learned from its campaign aimed at the US presidential election to future influence efforts in the United States and worldwide, including against US allies and their election processes. We assess the Russian intelligence services would have seen their election influence campaign as at least a qualified success because of their perceived ability to impact public discussion.

• Putin's public views of the disclosures suggest the Kremlin and the intelligence services will continue to consider using cyber-enabled disclosure operations because of their belief that these can accomplish Russian goals relatively easily without significant damage to Russian interests.

• Russia has sought to influence elections across Europe.

We assess Russian intelligence services will continue to develop capabilities to provide Putin with options to use against the United States, judging from past practice and current efforts. Immediately after Election Day, we assess Russian intelligence began a spearphishing campaign targeting US Government employees and individuals associated with US think tanks and NGOs in national security, defense, and foreign policy fields. This campaign could provide material for future influence efforts as well as foreign intelligence collection on the incoming administration's goals and plans.

Annex A
Russia -- Kremlin's TV Seeks To Influence Politics, Fuel Discontent in US

RT America TV, a Kremlin-financed channel operated from within the United States, has substantially expanded its repertoire of programming that highlights criticism of alleged US shortcomings in democracy and civil liberties. The rapid expansion of RT's operations and budget and recent candid statements by RT's leadership point to the channel's importance to the Kremlin as a messaging tool and indicate a Kremlin directed campaign to undermine faith in the US Government and fuel political protest.

The Kremlin has committed significant resources to expanding the channel's reach, particularly its social media footprint. A reliable UK report states that RT recently was the most-watched foreign news channel in the UK. RT America has positioned itself as a domestic US channel and has deliberately sought to obscure any legal ties to the Russian Government.

In the runup to the 2012 US presidential election in November, English-language channel RT America -- created and financed by the Russian Government and part of Russian Government-sponsored RT TV (see textbox 1) -- intensified its usually critical coverage of the United States. The channel portrayed the US electoral process as undemocratic and featured calls by US protesters for the public to rise up and 'take this government back.'

• RT introduced two new shows -- 'Breaking the Set' on 4 September and 'Truthseeker' on 2 November -- both overwhelmingly focused on criticism of US and Western governments as well as the promotion of radical discontent.

• From August to November 2012, RT ran numerous reports on alleged US election fraud and voting machine vulnerabilities, contending that US election results cannot be trusted and do not reflect the popular will.

• In an effort to highlight the alleged 'lack of democracy' in the United States, RT broadcast, hosted, and advertised thirdparty candidate debates and ran reporting supportive of the political agenda of these candidates. The RT hosts asserted that the US two-party system does not represent the views of at least one-third of the population and is a 'sham.'

RT aired a documentary about the Occupy Wall Street movement on 1, 2, and 4 November. RT framed the movement as a fight against 'the ruling class' and described the current US political system as corrupt and dominated by corporations. RT advertising for the documentary featured Occupy movement calls to 'take back' the government. The documentary claimed that the US system cannot be changed democratically, but only through 'revolution.' After the 6 November US presidential election, RT aired a documentary called 'Cultures of Protest,' about active and often violent political resistance (RT, 1-10 November).

RT Conducts Strategic Messaging
for Russian Government

RT's criticism of the US election was the latest facet of its broader and longer-standing anti-US messaging likely aimed at undermining viewers' trust in US democratic procedures and undercutting US criticism of Russia's political system. RT Editor in Chief Margarita Simonyan recently declared that the United States itself lacks democracy and that it has 'no moral right to teach the rest of the world' (Kommersant, 6 November).

• Simonyan has characterized RT's coverage of the Occupy Wall Street movement as 'information warfare' that is aimed at promoting popular dissatisfaction with the US Government. RT created a Facebook app to connect Occupy Wall Street protesters via social media. In addition, RT featured its own hosts in Occupy rallies ('Minaev Live,' 10 April; RT, 2, 12 June).

• RT's reports often characterize the United States as a 'surveillance state' and allege widespread infringements of civil liberties, police brutality, and drone use (RT, 24, 28 October, 1-10 November).

• RT has also focused on criticism of the US economic system, US currency policy, alleged Wall Street greed, and the US national debt. Some of RT's hosts have compared the United States to Imperial Rome and have predicted that government corruption and 'corporate greed' will lead to US financial collapse (RT, 31 October, 4 November).

RT broadcasts support for other Russian interests in areas such as foreign and energy policy.

• RT runs anti-fracking programming, highlighting environmental issues and the impacts on public health. This is likely reflective of the Russian Government's concern about the impact of fracking and US natural gas production on the global energy market and the potential challenges to Gazprom's profitability (5 October).

• RT is a leading media voice opposing Western intervention in the Syrian conflict and blaming the West for waging 'information wars' against the Syrian Government (RT, 10 October-9 November).

• In an earlier example of RT's messaging in support of the Russian Government, during the Georgia-Russia military conflict the channel accused Georgians of killing civilians and organizing a genocide of the Ossetian people. According to Simonyan, when 'the Ministry of Defense was at war with Georgia,' RT was 'waging an information war against the entire Western world' (Kommersant, 11 July).

In recent interviews, RT's leadership has candidly acknowledged its mission to expand its US audience and to expose it to Kremlin messaging. However, the leadership rejected claims that RT interferes in US domestic affairs.

• Simonyan claimed in popular arts magazine Afisha on 3 October: 'It is important to have a channel that people get used to, and then, when needed, you show them what you need to show. In some sense, not having our own foreign broadcasting is the same as not having a ministry of defense. When there is no war, it looks like we don't need it. However, when there is a war, it is critical.'

• According to Simonyan, 'the word 'propaganda' has a very negative connotation, but indeed, there is not a single international foreign TV channel that is doing something other than promotion of the values of the country that it is broadcasting from.' She added that 'when Russia is at war, we are, of course, on Russia's side' (Afisha, 3 October; Kommersant, 4 July).

• TV-Novosti director Nikolov said on 4 October to the Association of Cable Television that RT builds on worldwide demand for 'an alternative view of the entire world.' Simonyan asserted on 3 October in Afisha that RT's goal is 'to make an alternative channel that shares information unavailable elsewhere' in order to 'conquer the audience' and expose it to Russian state messaging (Afisha, 3 October; Kommersant, 4 July).

• On 26 May, Simonyan tweeted with irony: 'Ambassador McFaul hints that our channel is interference with US domestic affairs. And we, sinful souls, were thinking that it is freedom of speech.'

RT Leadership Closely Tied to, Controlled by Kremlin
RT Editor in Chief Margarita Simonyan has close ties to top Russian Government officials, especially Presidential Administration Deputy Chief of Staff Aleksey Gromov, who reportedly manages political TV coverage in Russia and is one of the founders of RT.

• Simonyan has claimed that Gromov shielded her from other officials and their requests to air certain reports. Russian media consider Simonyan to be Gromov's protege (Kommersant, 4 July; Dozhd TV, 11 July).

• Simonyan replaced Gromov on stateowned Channel One's Board of Directors. Government officials, including Gromov and Putin's Press Secretary Peskov were involved in creating RT and appointing Simonyan (Afisha, 3 October).

• According to Simonyan, Gromov oversees political coverage on TV, and he has periodic meetings with media managers where he shares classified information and discusses their coverage plans. Some opposition journalists, including Andrey Loshak, claim that he also ordered media attacks on opposition figures (Kommersant, 11 July). The Kremlin staffs RT and closely supervises RT's coverage, recruiting people who can convey Russian strategic messaging because of their ideological beliefs.

• The head of RT's Arabic-language service, Aydar Aganin, was rotated from the diplomatic service to manage RT's Arabic-language expansion, suggesting a close relationship between RT and Russia's foreign policy apparatus. RT's London Bureau is managed by Darya Pushkova, the daughter of Aleksey Pushkov, the current chair of the Duma Russian Foreign Affairs Committee and a former Gorbachev speechwriter (DXB, 26 March 2009; MK.ru, 13 March 2006).

• According to Simonyan, the Russian Government sets rating and viewership requirements for RT and, 'since RT receives budget from the state, it must complete tasks given by the state.' According to Nikolov, RT news stories are written and edited 'to become news' exclusively in RT's Moscow office (Dozhd TV, 11 July; AKT, 4 October).

• In her interview with pro-Kremlin journalist Sergey Minaev, Simonyan complimented RT staff in the United States for passionately defending Russian positions on the air and in social media. Simonyan said: 'I wish you could see...how these guys, not just on air, but on their own social networks, Twitter, and when giving interviews, how they defend the positions that we stand on!' ('Minaev Live,' 10 April).

RT Focuses on Social Media, Building Audience

RT aggressively advertises its social media accounts and has a significant and fast-growing social media footprint. In line with its efforts to present itself as anti-mainstream and to provide viewers alternative news content, RT is making its social media operations a top priority, both to avoid broadcast TV regulations and to expand its overall audience.

• According to RT management, RT's website receives at least 500,000 unique viewers every day. Since its inception in 2005, RT videos received more than 800 million views on YouTube (1 million views per day), which is the highest among news outlets (see graphics for comparison with other news channels) (AKT, 4 October).

• According to Simonyan, the TV audience worldwide is losing trust in traditional TV broadcasts and stations, while the popularity of 'alternative channels' like RT or Al Jazeera grows. RT markets itself as an 'alternative channel' that is available via the Internet everywhere in the world, and it encourages interaction and social networking (Kommersant, 29 September).

• According to Simonyan, RT uses social media to expand the reach of its political reporting and uses well-trained people to monitor public opinion in social media commentaries (Kommersant, 29 September).

• According to Nikolov, RT requires its hosts to have social media accounts, in part because social media allows the distribution of content that would not be allowed on television (Newreporter.org, 11 October).

• Simonyan claimed in her 3 October interview to independent TV channel Dozhd that Occupy Wall Street coverage gave RT a significant audience boost.

The Kremlin spends $190 million a year on the distribution and dissemination of RT programming, focusing on hotels and satellite, terrestrial, and cable broadcasting. The Kremlin is rapidly expanding RT's availability around the world and giving it a reach comparable to channels such as Al Jazeera English. According to Simonyan, the United Kingdom and the United States are RT's most successful markets. RT does not, however, publish audience information.

• According to market research company Nielsen, RT had the most rapid growth (40 percent) among all international news channels in the United States over the past year (2012). Its audience in New York tripled and in Washington DC grew by 60% (Kommersant, 4 July).

• RT claims that it is surpassing Al Jazeera in viewership in New York and Washington DC (BARB, 20 November; RT, 21 November).

• RT states on its website that it can reach more than 550 million people worldwide and 85 million people in the United States; however, it does not publicize its actual US audience numbers (RT, 10 December).

Formal Disassociation From Kremlin Facilitates RT US Messaging

RT America formally disassociates itself from the Russian Government by using a Moscow-based autonomous nonprofit organization to finance its US operations. According to RT's leadership, this structure was set up to avoid the Foreign Agents Registration Act and to facilitate licensing abroad. In addition, RT rebranded itself in 2008 to deemphasize its Russian origin.

• According to Simonyan, RT America differs from other Russian state institutions in terms of ownership, but not in terms of financing. To disassociate RT from the Russian Government, the federal news agency RIA Novosti established a subsidiary autonomous nonprofit organization, TVNovosti, using the formal independence of this company to establish and finance RT worldwide (Dozhd TV, 11 July).

• Nikolov claimed that RT is an 'autonomous noncommercial entity,' which is 'well received by foreign regulators' and 'simplifies getting a license.' Simonyan said that RT America is not a 'foreign agent' according to US law because it uses a US commercial organization for its broadcasts (AKT, 4 October; Dozhd TV, 11 July).

• Simonyan observed that RT's original Russia-centric news reporting did not generate sufficient audience, so RT switched to covering international and US domestic affairs and removed the words 'Russia Today' from the logo 'to stop scaring away the audience' (Afisha, 18 October; Kommersant, 4 July).

• RT hires or makes contractual agreements with Westerners with views that fit its agenda and airs them on RT. Simonyan said on the pro-Kremlin show 'Minaev Live' on 10 April that RT has enough audience and money to be able to choose its hosts, and it chooses the hosts that 'think like us,' 'are interested in working in the anti-mainstream,' and defend RT's beliefs on social media. Some hosts and journalists do not present themselves as associated with RT when interviewing people, and many of them have affiliations to other media and activist organizations in the United States ('Minaev Live,' 10 April).

SOURCE 4

https://wikileaks.org/ciav7p1/

Vault 7: CIA Hacking Tools Revealed
Press Release

Today, Tuesday 7 March 2017, WikiLeaks begins its new series of leaks on the U.S. Central Intelligence Agency. Code-named 'Vault 7' by WikiLeaks, it is the largest ever publication of confidential documents on the agency.

The first full part of the series, 'Year Zero,' comprises 8,761 documents and files from an isolated, high-security network situated inside the CIA's Center for Cyber Intelligence in Langley, Virginia. It follows an introductory disclosure last month of CIA targeting French political parties and candidates in the lead up to the 2012 presidential election.

Recently, the CIA lost control of the majority of its hacking arsenal including malware, viruses, trojans, weaponized 'zero day' exploits, malware remote control systems and associated documentation. This extraordinary collection, which amounts to more than several hundred million lines of code, gives its possessor the entire hacking capacity of the CIA. The archive appears to have been circulated among former U.S. government hackers and contractors in an unauthorized manner, one of whom has provided WikiLeaks with portions of the archive.

'Year Zero' introduces the scope and direction of the CIA's global covert hacking program, its malware arsenal and dozens of 'zero day' weaponized exploits against a wide range of U.S. and European company products, include Apple's iPhone, Google's Android and Microsoft's Windows and even Samsung TVs, which are turned into covert microphones.

Since 2001 the CIA has gained political and budgetary preeminence over the U.S. National Security Agency (NSA). The CIA found itself building not just its now infamous drone fleet, but a very different type of covert, globe-spanning force — its own substantial fleet of hackers. The agency's hacking division freed it from having to disclose its often controversial operations to the NSA (its primary bureaucratic rival) in order to draw on the NSA's hacking capacities.

By the end of 2016, the CIA's hacking division, which formally falls under the agency's Center for Cyber Intelligence (CCI), had over 5000 registered users and had produced more than a thousand hacking systems, trojans, viruses, and other 'weaponized' malware. Such is the scale of the CIA's undertaking that by 2016, its hackers had utilized more code than that used to run Facebook. The CIA had created, in effect, its 'own NSA' with even less accountability and without publicly answering the question as to whether such a massive budgetary spend on duplicating the capacities of a rival agency could be justified.

In a statement to WikiLeaks the source details policy questions that they say urgently need to be debated in public, including whether the CIA's hacking capabilities exceed its mandated powers and the problem of public oversight of the agency. The source wishes to initiate a public debate about the security, creation, use, proliferation and democratic control of cyberweapons.

Once a single cyber 'weapon' is 'loose' it can spread around the world in seconds, to be used by rival states, cyber mafia and teenage hackers alike.

Julian Assange, WikiLeaks editor stated that 'There is an extreme proliferation risk in the development of cyber 'weapons.' Comparisons can be drawn between the uncontrolled proliferation of such 'weapons,' which results from the inability to contain them combined with their high market value, and the global arms trade. But the significance of 'Year Zero' goes well beyond the choice between cyberwar and cyberpeace. The disclosure is also exceptional from a political, legal and forensic perspective.'

Wikileaks has carefully reviewed the 'Year Zero' disclosure and published substantive CIA documentation while avoiding the distribution of 'armed' cyberweapons until a consensus emerges on the technical and political nature of the CIA's program and how such 'weapons' should analyzed, disarmed and published.

Wikileaks has also decided to redact and anonymise some identifying information in 'Year Zero' for in depth analysis. These redactions include tens of thousands of CIA targets and attack machines throughout Latin America, Europe and the United States. While we are aware of the imperfect results of any approach chosen, we remain committed to our publishing model and note that the quantity of published pages in 'Vault 7' part one ('Year Zero') already eclipses the total number of pages published over the first three years of the Edward Snowden NSA leaks.

Analysis

CIA malware targets iPhone, Android, smart TVs

CIA malware and hacking tools are built by EDG (Engineering Development Group), a software development group within CCI

(Center for Cyber Intelligence), a department belonging to the CIA's DDI (Directorate for Digital Innovation). The DDI is one of the five major directorates of the CIA (see this organizational chart of the CIA for more details).

The EDG is responsible for the development, testing and operational support of all backdoors, exploits, malicious payloads, trojans, viruses and any other kind of malware used by the CIA in its covert operations world-wide.

The increasing sophistication of surveillance techniques has drawn comparisons with George Orwell's 1984, but 'Weeping Angel,' developed by the CIA's Embedded Devices Branch (EDB), which infests smart TVs, transforming them into covert microphones, is surely its most emblematic realization.

The attack against Samsung smart TVs was developed in cooperation with the United Kingdom's MI5/BTSS. After infestation, Weeping Angel places the target TV in a 'Fake-Off' mode, so that the owner falsely believes the TV is off when it is on. In 'Fake-Off' mode the TV operates as a bug, recording conversations in the room and sending them over the Internet to a covert CIA server.

As of October 2014 the CIA was also looking at infecting the vehicle control systems used by modern cars and trucks. The purpose of such control is not specified, but it would permit the CIA to engage in nearly undetectable assassinations.

The CIA's Mobile Devices Branch (MDB) developed numerous attacks to remotely hack and control popular smart phones. Infected phones can be instructed to send the CIA the user's geolocation, audio and text communications as well as covertly activate the phone's camera and microphone.

Despite iPhone's minority share (14.5%) of the global smart phone market in 2016, a specialized unit in the CIA's Mobile Development Branch produces malware to infest, control and exfiltrate data from iPhones and other Apple products running iOS, such as iPads. CIA's arsenal includes numerous local and remote 'zero days' developed by CIA or obtained from GCHQ, NSA, FBI or purchased from cyber arms contractors such as Baitshop. The disproportionate focus on iOS may be explained by the popularity of the iPhone among social, political, diplomatic and business elites.

A similar unit targets Google's Android which is used to run the majority of the world's smart phones (~85%) including Samsung, HTC and Sony. 1.15 billion Android powered phones were sold last year. 'Year Zero' shows that as of 2016 the CIA had 24 'weaponized' Android 'zero days' which it has developed itself and obtained from GCHQ, NSA and cyber arms contractors.

These techniques permit the CIA to bypass the encryption of WhatsApp, Signal, Telegram, Wiebo, Confide and Cloackman by hacking the 'smart' phones that they run on and collecting audio and message traffic before encryption is applied.

CIA malware targets Windows, OSx, Linux, routers

The CIA also runs a very substantial effort to infect and control Microsoft Windows users with its malware. This includes multiple local and remote weaponized 'zero days,' air gap jumping viruses such as 'Hammer Drill' which infects software distributed on CD/DVDs, infectors for removable media such as USBs, systems to hide data in images or in covert disk areas ('Brutal Kangaroo') and to keep its malware infestations going.

Many of these infection efforts are pulled together by the CIA's Automated Implant Branch (AIB), which has developed several attack systems for automated infestation and control of CIA malware, such as 'Assassin' and 'Medusa.'

Attacks against Internet infrastructure and webservers are developed by the CIA's Network Devices Branch (NDB).

The CIA has developed automated multi-platform malware attack and control systems covering Windows, Mac OS X, Solaris, Linux and more, such as EDB's 'HIVE' and the related 'Cutthroat' and 'Swindle' tools, which are described in the examples section below.

CIA 'hoarded' vulnerabilities ('zero days')

In the wake of Edward Snowden's leaks about the NSA, the U.S. technology industry secured a commitment from the Obama administration that the executive would disclose on an ongoing basis — rather than hoard — serious vulnerabilities, exploits, bugs or 'zero days' to Apple, Google, Microsoft, and other US-based manufacturers.

Serious vulnerabilities not disclosed to the manufacturers places huge swathes of the population and critical infrastructure at risk to foreign intelligence or cyber criminals who independently discover or hear rumors of the vulnerability. If the CIA can discover such vulnerabilities so can others.

The U.S. government's commitment to the Vulnerabilities Equities Process came after significant lobbying by US technology companies, who risk losing their share of the global market over real and perceived hidden vulnerabilities. The government stated that it would disclose all pervasive vulnerabilities discovered after 2010 on an ongoing basis.

'Year Zero' documents show that the CIA breached the Obama administration's commitments. Many of the vulnerabilities used in the CIA's cyber arsenal are pervasive and some may already have been found by rival intelligence agencies or cyber criminals.

As an example, specific CIA malware revealed in 'Year Zero' is able to penetrate, infest and control both the Android phone and iPhone software that runs or has run presidential Twitter accounts. The CIA attacks this software by using undisclosed security vulnerabilities ('zero days') possessed by the CIA but if the CIA can hack these phones then so can everyone else who has obtained or discovered the vulnerability. As long as the CIA keeps these vulnerabilities concealed from Apple and Google (who make the phones) they will not be fixed, and the phones will remain hackable.

The same vulnerabilities exist for the population at large, including the U.S. Cabinet, Congress, top CEOs, system administrators, security officers and engineers. By hiding these security flaws from manufacturers like Apple and Google the CIA ensures that it can hack everyone; at the expense of leaving everyone hackable.

'Cyberwar' programs are a serious proliferation risk

Cyber 'weapons' are not possible to keep under effective control.

While nuclear proliferation has been restrained by the enormous costs and visible infrastructure involved in assembling enough fissile material to produce a critical nuclear mass, cyber 'weapons,' once developed, are very hard to retain.

Cyber 'weapons' are in fact just computer programs which can be pirated like any other. Since they are entirely comprised of information they can be copied quickly with no marginal cost.

Securing such 'weapons' is particularly difficult since the same people who develop and use them have the skills to exfiltrate copies without leaving traces — sometimes by using the very same 'weapons' against the organizations that contain them. There are substantial price incentives for government hackers and consultants to obtain copies since there is a global 'vulnerability market' that will pay hundreds of thousands to millions of dollars for copies of such 'weapons.' Similarly, contractors and companies who obtain such 'weapons' sometimes use them for their own purposes, obtaining advantage over their competitors in selling 'hacking' services.

Over the last three years the United States intelligence sector, which consists of government agencies such as the CIA and NSA and their contractors, such as Booz Allan Hamilton, has been subject to unprecedented series of data exfiltrations by its own workers.

A number of intelligence community members not yet publicly named have been arrested or subject to federal criminal investigations in separate incidents.
Most visibly, on February 8, 2017 a U.S. federal grand jury indicted Harold T. Martin III with 20 counts of mishandling classified information. The Department of Justice alleged that it seized some 50,000 gigabytes of information from Harold T. Martin III that he had obtained from classified programs at NSA and CIA, including the source code for numerous hacking tools.

Once a single cyber 'weapon' is 'loose' it can spread around the world in seconds, to be used by peer states, cyber mafia and teenage hackers alike.

U.S. Consulate in Frankfurt is a covert CIA hacker base

In addition to its operations in Langley, Virginia the CIA also uses the U.S. consulate in Frankfurt as a covert base for its hackers covering Europe, the Middle East and Africa.

CIA hackers operating out of the Frankfurt consulate ('Center for Cyber Intelligence Europe' or CCIE) are given diplomatic ('black') passports and State Department cover.

The instructions for incoming CIA hackers make Germany's counter-intelligence efforts appear inconsequential: 'Breeze through German Customs because you have your cover-for-action story down pat, and all they did was stamp your passport'

Your Cover Story (for this trip)

Q: Why are you here?
A: Supporting technical consultations at the Consulate.
Two earlier WikiLeaks publications give further detail on CIA approaches to customs and secondary screening procedures.

Once in Frankfurt CIA hackers can travel without further border checks to the 25 European countries that are part of the Schengen open border area — including France, Italy and Switzerland.

A number of the CIA's electronic attack methods are designed for physical proximity. These attack methods are able to penetrate high security networks that are disconnected from the internet, such as police record database. In these cases, a CIA officer, agent or allied intelligence officer acting under instructions, physically infiltrates the targeted workplace.

The attacker is provided with a USB containing malware developed for the CIA for this purpose, which is inserted into the targeted computer. The attacker then infects and exfiltrates data to removable media. For example, the CIA attack system Fine Dining, provides 24 decoy applications for CIA spies to use. To witnesses, the spy appears to be running a program showing videos (e.g VLC), presenting slides (Prezi), playing a computer game (Breakout2, 2048) or even running a fake virus scanner (Kaspersky, McAfee, Sophos). But while the decoy application is on the screen, the underlaying system is automatically infected and ransacked.

How the CIA dramatically increased proliferation risks

In what is surely one of the most astounding intelligence own goals in living memory, the CIA structured its classification regime such that for the most market valuable part of 'Vault 7' — the CIA's weaponized malware (implants + zero days), Listening Posts (LP), and Command and Control (C2) systems — the agency has little legal recourse.

The CIA made these systems unclassified

Why the CIA chose to make its cyberarsenal unclassified reveals how concepts developed for military use do not easily crossover to the 'battlefield' of cyber 'war.'

To attack its targets, the CIA usually requires that its implants communicate with their control programs over the internet. If CIA implants, Command & Control and Listening Post software were classified, then CIA officers could be prosecuted or dismissed for violating rules that prohibit placing classified information onto the Internet. Consequently the CIA has secretly made most of its cyber spying/war code unclassified. The U.S. government is not able to assert copyright either, due to restrictions in the U.S. Constitution. This means that cyber 'arms' manufacturers and computer hackers can freely 'pirate' these 'weapons' if they are obtained. The CIA has primarily had to rely on obfuscation to protect its malware secrets.

Conventional weapons such as missiles may be fired at the enemy (i.e. into an unsecured area). Proximity to or impact with the target detonates the ordnance including its classified parts. Hence military personnel do not violate classification rules by firing ordnance with classified parts. Ordnance will likely explode. If it does not, that is not the operator's intent.

Over the last decade U.S. hacking operations have been increasingly dressed up in military jargon to tap into Department of Defense funding streams. For instance, attempted 'malware injections' (commercial jargon) or 'implant drops' (NSA jargon) are being called 'fires' as if a weapon was being fired. However the analogy is questionable.

Unlike bullets, bombs or missiles, most CIA malware is designed to live for days or even years after it has reached its 'target.' CIA malware does not 'explode on impact' but rather permanently infests its target. In order to infect target's device, copies of the malware must be placed on the target's devices, giving physical possession of the malware to the target. To exfiltrate data back to the CIA or to await further instructions the malware must communicate with CIA Command & Control (C2) systems placed on internet connected servers. But such servers are typically not approved to hold classified information, so CIA command and control systems are also made unclassified.

A successful 'attack' on a target's computer system is more like a series of complex stock maneuvers in a hostile take-over bid or the careful planting of rumors in order to gain control over an organization's leadership rather than the firing of a weapons system. If there is a military analogy to be made, the infestation of a target is perhaps akin to the execution of a whole series of military maneuvers against the target's territory including observation, infiltration, occupation and exploitation.

Evading forensics and anti-virus

A series of standards lay out CIA malware infestation patterns which are likely to assist forensic crime scene investigators as well as Apple, Microsoft, Google, Samsung, Nokia, Blackberry, Siemens and anti-virus companies attribute and defend against attacks.

'Tradecraft DO's and DON'Ts' contains CIA rules on how its malware should be written to avoid fingerprints implicating the 'CIA, US government, or its witting partner companies' in 'forensic review.' Similar secret standards cover the use of encryption to hide CIA hacker and malware communication (pdf), describing targets & exfiltrated data (pdf) as well as executing payloads (pdf) and persisting (pdf) in the target's machines over time.

CIA hackers developed successful attacks against most well known anti-virus programs. These are documented in AV defeats, Personal Security Products, Detecting and defeating PSPs and PSP/Debugger/RE Avoidance. For example, Comodo was defeated by CIA malware placing itself in the Window's 'Recycle Bin.' While Comodo 6.x has a 'Gaping Hole of DOOM.'
CIA hackers discussed what the NSA's 'Equation Group' hackers did wrong and how the CIA's malware makers could avoid similar exposure.

Examples

The CIA's Engineering Development Group (EDG) management system contains around 500 different projects (only some of which are documented by 'Year Zero') each with their own sub-projects, malware and hacker tools.

The majority of these projects relate to tools that are used for penetration, infestation ('implanting'), control, and exfiltration.

Another branch of development focuses on the development and operation of Listening Posts (LP) and Command and Control (C2) systems used to communicate with and control CIA implants; special projects are used to target specific hardware from routers to smart TVs.
Some example projects are described below, but see the table of contents for the full list of projects described by WikiLeaks' 'Year Zero.'

UMBRAGE

The CIA's hand crafted hacking techniques pose a problem for the agency. Each technique it has created forms a 'fingerprint' that can be used by forensic investigators to attribute multiple different attacks to the same entity.

This is analogous to finding the same distinctive knife wound on multiple separate murder victims. The unique wounding style creates suspicion that a single murderer is responsible. As soon one murder in the set is solved then the other murders also find likely attribution.

The CIA's Remote Devices Branch's UMBRAGE group collects and maintains a substantial library of attack techniques 'stolen' from malware produced in other states including the Russian Federation.

With UMBRAGE and related projects the CIA cannot only increase its total number of attack types but also misdirect attribution by leaving behind the 'fingerprints' of the groups that the attack techniques were stolen from.

UMBRAGE components cover keyloggers, password collection, webcam capture, data destruction, persistence, privilege escalation, stealth, anti-virus (PSP) avoidance and survey techniques.

Fine Dining

Fine Dining comes with a standardized questionnaire i.e. menu that CIA case officers fill out. The questionnaire is used by the agency's OSB (Operational Support Branch) to transform the requests of case officers into technical requirements for hacking attacks (typically 'exfiltrating' information from computer systems) for specific operations. The questionnaire allows the OSB to identify how to adapt existing tools for the operation, and communicate this to CIA malware configuration staff. The OSB functions as the interface between CIA operational staff and the relevant technical support staff.

Among the list of possible targets of the collection are 'Asset,' 'Liason Asset,' 'System Administrator,' 'Foreign Information Operations,' 'Foreign Intelligence Agencies' and 'Foreign Government Entities.' Notably absent is any reference to extremists or transnational criminals. The 'Case Officer' is also asked to specify the environment of the target like the type of computer, operating system used, Internet connectivity and installed anti-virus utilities (PSPs) as well as a list of file types to be exfiltrated like Office documents, audio, video, images or custom file types. The 'menu' also asks for information if recurring access to the target is possible and how long unobserved access to the computer can be maintained. This information is used by the CIA's 'JQJIMPROVISE' software (see below) to configure a set of CIA malware suited to the specific needs of an operation.

Improvise (JQJIMPROVISE)

'Improvise' is a toolset for configuration, post-processing, payload setup and execution vector selection for survey/exfiltration tools supporting all major operating systems like Windows (Bartender), MacOS (JukeBox) and Linux (DanceFloor). Its configuration utilities like Margarita allows the NOC (Network Operation Center) to customize tools based on requirements from 'Fine Dining' questionnaires.

HIVE

HIVE is a multi-platform CIA malware suite and its associated control software. The project provides customizable implants for Windows, Solaris, MikroTik (used in internet routers) and Linux platforms and a Listening Post (LP)/Command and Control (C2) infrastructure to communicate with these implants.

The implants are configured to communicate via HTTPS with the webserver of a cover domain; each operation utilizing these implants has a separate cover domain and the infrastructure can handle any number of cover domains.

Each cover domain resolves to an IP address that is located at a commercial VPS (Virtual Private Server) provider. The public-facing server forwards all incoming traffic via a VPN to a 'Blot' server that handles actual connection requests from clients. It is setup for optional SSL client authentication: if a client sends a valid client certificate (only implants can do that), the connection is forwarded to the 'Honeycomb' toolserver that communicates with the implant; if a valid certificate is missing (which is the case if someone tries to open the cover domain website by accident), the traffic is forwarded to a cover server that delivers an unsuspicious looking website.

The Honeycomb toolserver receives exfiltrated information from the implant; an operator can also task the implant to execute jobs on the target computer, so the toolserver acts as a C2 (command and control) server for the implant.

Similar functionality (though limited to Windows) is provided by the RickBobby project.

See the classified user and developer guides for HIVE.

Frequently Asked Questions

Why now?

WikiLeaks published as soon as its verification and analysis were ready.

In February the Trump administration has issued an Executive Order calling for a 'Cyberwar' review to be prepared within 30 days.

While the review increases the timeliness and relevance of the publication it did not play a role in setting the publication date.

Redactions

Names, email addresses and external IP addresses have been redacted in the released pages (70,875 redactions in total) until further analysis is complete.

1. **Over-redaction:** Some items may have been redacted that are not employees, contractors, targets or otherwise related to the agency, but are, for example, authors of documentation for otherwise public projects that are used by the agency.
2. **Identity vs. person:** the redacted names are replaced by user IDs (numbers) to allow readers to assign multiple pages to a single author. Given the redaction process used a single person may be represented by more than one assigned identifier but no identifier refers to more than one real person.
3. **Archive attachments (zip, tar.gz, ...)** are replaced with a PDF listing all the file names in the archive. As the archive content is assessed it may be made available; until then the archive is redacted.
4. **Attachments with other binary content** are replaced by a hex dump of the content to prevent accidental invocation of binaries that may have been infected with weaponized CIA malware. As the content is assessed it may be made available; until then the content is redacted.
5. **The tens of thousands of routable IP addresses references** (including more than 22 thousand within the United States) that correspond to possible targets, CIA covert listening post servers, intermediary and test systems, are redacted for further exclusive investigation.
6. **Binary files of non-public origin** are only available as dumps to prevent accidental invocation of CIA malware infected binaries.

Organizational Chart

The organizational chart corresponds to the material published by WikiLeaks so far.

Since the organizational structure of the CIA below the level of Directorates is not public, the placement of the EDG and its branches within the org chart of the agency is reconstructed from information contained in the documents released so far. It is intended to be used as a rough outline of the internal organization; please be aware that the reconstructed org chart is incomplete and that internal reorganizations occur frequently.

Wiki Pages

'Year Zero' contains 7818 web pages with 943 attachments from the internal development groupware. The software used for this purpose is called Confluence, a proprietary software from Atlassian. Webpages in this system (like in Wikipedia) have a version history that can provide interesting insights on how a document evolved over time; the 7818 documents include these page histories for 1136 latest versions.

The order of named pages within each level is determined by date (oldest first). Page content is not present if it was originally dynamically created by the Confluence software (as indicated on the re-constructed page).

What time period is covered?

The years 2013 to 2016. The sort order of the pages within each level is determined by date (oldest first).
WikiLeaks has obtained the CIA's creation/last modification date for each page, but these do not yet appear for technical reasons. Usually the date can be discerned or approximated from the content and the page order. If it is critical to know the exact time/ date contact WikiLeaks.

What is 'Vault 7'
'Vault 7' is a substantial collection of material about CIA activities obtained by WikiLeaks.

When was each part of 'Vault 7' obtained?
Part one was obtained recently and covers through 2016. Details on the other parts will be available at the time of publication.

Is each part of 'Vault 7' from a different source?
Details on the other parts will be available at the time of publication.

What is the total size of 'Vault 7'?
The series is the largest intelligence publication in history.

How did WikiLeaks obtain each part of 'Vault 7'?
Sources trust WikiLeaks to not reveal information that might help identify them.

Isn't WikiLeaks worried that the CIA will act against its staff to stop the series?
No. That would be certainly counter-productive.

Has WikiLeaks already 'mined' all the best stories?
No. WikiLeaks has intentionally not written up hundreds of impactful stories to encourage others to find them and so create expertise in the area for subsequent parts in the series. They're there. Look. Those who demonstrate journalistic excellence may be considered for early access to future parts.

Won't other journalists find all the best stories before me?
Unlikely. There are very considerably more stories than there are journalists or academics who are in a position to write them.

SOURCE 5

https://www.treasury.gov/resource-center/sanctions/
Programs/Documents/cyber2_eo.pdf

Presidential Documents

**Executive Order 13757 of December 28, 2016 Taking
Additional Steps to Address the National Emergency With
Respect to Significant Malicious Cyber-Enabled Activities**

By the authority vested in me as President by the Constitution and the laws of the United States of America, including the International Emergency Economic Powers Act (50 U.S.C. 1701 et seq.) (IEEPA), the National Emergencies Act (50 U.S.C. 1601 et seq.) (NEA), and section 301 of title 3, United States Code, I, BARACK OBAMA, President of the United States of America, in order to take additional steps to deal with the national emergency with respect to significant malicious cyber-enabled activities declared in Executive Order 13694 of April 1, 2015, and in view of the increasing use of such activities to undermine democratic processes or institutions, hereby order: Section 1.

Section 1(a) of Executive Order 13694 is hereby amended to read as follows: "Section 1. (a) All property and interests in property that are in the United States, that hereafter come within the United States, or that are or hereafter come within the possession or control of any United States person of the following persons are blocked and may not be transferred, paid, exported, withdrawn, or otherwise dealt in: (i) the persons listed in the Annex to this order; (ii) any person determined by the Secretary of the Treasury, in consultation with the Attorney General and the Secretary of State, to be responsible for or complicit in, or to have engaged in, directly or indirectly, cyber-enabled activities originating from, or directed by persons located, in whole or in substantial part, outside the United States that are reasonably likely to result in, or have materially contributed to, a significant threat to the national security, foreign policy, or economic health or financial stability of the United States and that have the purpose or effect of: (A) harming, or otherwise significantly compromising the provision of services by, a computer or network of computers that support one or more entities in a critical infrastructure sector; (B) significantly compromising the provision of services by one or more entities in a critical infrastructure sector; (C) causing a significant disruption to the availability of a computer or network of computers; (D) causing a significant misappropriation of funds or economic resources, trade secrets, personal identifiers, or financial information for commercial or competitive advantage or private financial gain; or (E) tampering with, altering, or causing a misappropriation of information with the purpose or effect of interfering with or undermining election processes or institutions; and (iii) any person determined by the Secretary of the Treasury, in consultation with the Attorney General and the Secretary of State: (A) to be responsible for or complicit in, or to have engaged in, the receipt or use for commercial or competitive advantage or private financial gain, or by a commercial entity, outside the United States of trade secrets misappropriated through cyber-enabled means, knowing they have been misappropriated, where the misappropriation of such trade secrets is reasonably likely to result in, or has materially contributed to, a significant threat to the national security, foreign policy, or economy of the United States; (B) to have materially assisted, sponsored, or provided financial, material, or technological support for, or goods or services to or in support of, any activity described in subsections (a)(ii) or (a)(iii)(A) of this section or any person whose property and interests in property are blocked pursuant to this order; (C) to be owned or controlled by, or to have acted or purported to act for or on behalf of, directly or indirectly, any person whose property and interests in property are blocked pursuant to this order; or (D) to have attempted to engage in any of the activities described in subsections (a)(ii) and (a)(iii)(A)–(C) of this section."

Sec. 2. Executive Order 13694 is further amended by adding as an Annex to Executive Order 13694 the Annex to this order.

Sec. 3. Executive Order 13694 is further amended by redesignating section 10 as section 11 and adding a new section 10 to read as follows: "Sec. 10. The Secretary of the Treasury, in consultation with the Attorney General and the Secretary of State, is hereby authorized to determine that circumstances no longer warrant the blocking of the property and interests in property of a person listed in the Annex to this order, and to take necessary action to give effect to that determination."

Sec. 4. This order is not intended to, and does not, create any right or benefit, substantive or procedural, enforceable at law or in equity by any party against the United States, its departments, agencies, or entities, its officers, employees, or agents, or any other person.

Sec. 5. This order is effective at 12:01 a.m. eastern standard time on December 29, 2016.

Entities

1. Main Intelligence Directorate (a.k.a. Glavnoe Razvedyvatel'noe Upravlenie) (a.k.a. GRU); Moscow, Russia
2. Federal Security Service (a.k.a. Federalnaya Sluzhba Bezopasnosti) (a.k.a FSB); Moscow, Russia

3. Special Technology Center (a.k.a. STLC, Ltd. Special Technology Center St. Petersburg); St. Petersburg, Russia
4. Zorsecurity (a.k.a. Esage Lab); Moscow, Russia
5. Autonomous Noncommercial Organization 'Professional Association of Designers of Data Processing Systems' (a.k.a. ANO PO KSI); Moscow, Russia

Individuals

1. Igor Valentinovich Korobov; DOB Aug 3, 1956; nationality, Russian
2. Sergey Aleksandrovich Gizunov; DOB Oct 18, 1956; nationality, Russian
3. Igor Olegovich Kostyukov; DOB Feb 21, 1961; nationality, Russian
4. Vladimir Stepanovich Alexseyev; DOB Apr 24, 1961; nationality, Russian

SOURCE 6

https://wikileaks.org/clinton-emails/

Hillary Clinton Email Archive

On March 16, 2016 WikiLeaks launched a searchable archive for over 30 thousand emails & email attachments sent to and from Hillary Clinton's private email server while she was Secretary of State.

The 50,547 pages of documents span from 30 June 2010 to 12 August 2014. 7,570 of the documents were sent by Hillary Clinton. The emails were made available in the form of thousands of PDFs by the US State Department as a result of a Freedom of Information Act request. More PDFs were made available on February 29, 2016, and a set of additional 995 emails was imported up to February 2, 2018.

SOURCES CONSULTED

[i]   https://www.thenation.com/article/how-did-russiagate-begin/

[ii]   https://www.theguardian.com/us-news/2016/nov/10/simpsons-predicted-president-trump-back-to-the-future

[iii]   https://www.breitbart.com/politics/2016/06/13/horowitz-donald-trumps-speech-game-changer/

[iv]   https://twitter.com/realDonaldTrump/status/743488055240196096

[v]   https://www.facebook.com/DonaldTrump/posts/10157169523180725

[vi]   https://twitter.com/JeffreyGuterman/status/743496282895900672

[vii]   https://twitter.com/JeffreyGuterman/status/1138923683290988545

[viii]   https://twitter.com/JeffreyGuterman/status/1138798866273226753

[ix] https://twitter.com/SpinDr/status/743488512247267330

[x]   https://edition.cnn.com/2016/11/07/politics/political-prediction-market-hillary-clinton-donald-trump/index.html

[xi] https://twitter.com/atrupar/status/743489416497356801

[xii]   https://twitter.com/THEMOCOLLINS/status/743537058069676032

[xiii]   https://www.nytimes.com/2016/12/13/us/politics/russia-hack-election-dnc.html

[xiv] https://www.politifact.com/truth-o-meter/statements/2016/aug/28/reince-priebus/did-hillary-clinton-call-african-american-youth-su/

[xv] https://www.washingtontimes.com/news/2016/mar/16/hillary-clintons-email-archive-made-searchable-wik/

[xvi] https://wikileaks.org/clinton-emails/

[xvii] https://www.buzzfeednews.com/article/sheerafrenkel/meet-fancy-bear-the-russian-group-hacking-the-us-election

[xviii] motherboard.vice.com/read/how-hackers-broke-into-john-podesta-and-colin-powells-gmail-accounts?trk_source=homepage-lede

[xix] https://www.wired.com/story/dnc-lawsuit-reveals-key-details-2016-hack/

[xx] https://www.nytimes.com/2016/12/13/us/politics/house-democrats-hacking-dccc.html

[xxi] https://obamawhitehouse.archives.gov/the-press-office/2016/04/13/president-obama-announces-more-key-administration-posts

[xxii] https://dailycaller.com/2017/06/24/crowdstrike-five-things-everyone-is-ignoring-about-the-russia-dnc-story/

[xxiii] https://www.dailymail.co.uk/news/article-4376628/New-questions-claim-Russia-hacked-election.html#ixzz4iZEpGDmk

[xxiv] https://www.washingtonexaminer.com/news/mueller-says-russias-gru-stole-clinton-dnc-emails-and-gave-them-to-wikileaks

[xxv] https://www.vox.com/2018/2/27/17060132/intelligence-russia-hacking-us-elections

[xxvi] https://www.theguardian.com/us-news/2016/apr/12/barack-obama-says-libya-was-worst-mistake-of-his-presidency

[xxvii] https://twitter.com/McFaul/status/850423127456665600

[xxviii] https://twitter.com/justinamash/status/985657911673344000

[xxix] https://twitter.com/ABMurage/status/933962754704080897

[xxx] https://www.theguardian.com/uk-news/2016/jul/06/mi6-stood-by-bogus-intelligence-until-after-iraq-invasion

[xxxi] https://www.theguardian.com/uk-news/2018/mar/02/mi5-agents-are-allowed-to-commit-in-uk-government-reveals

[xxxii] https://www.documentcloud.org/documents/3259984-Trump-Intelligence-Allegations.html

[xxxiii] https://www.buzzfeednews.com/article/kenbensinger/these-reports-allege-trump-has-deep-ties-to-russia

[xxxiv] https://www.theguardian.com/us-news/2018/jan/10/trump-lawyer-michael-cohen-sues-buzzfeed-russia-dossier

[xxxv] https://twitter.com/MichaelCohen212/status/950900224087724037

[xxxvi] https://www.breitbart.com/the-media/2019/06/12/death-spiral-continues-cnn-loses-one-third-primetime-audience/

[xxxvii] https://twitter.com/realDonaldTrump/status/818990655418617856

[xxxviii] https://time.com/5565991/russia-influence-2016-election/

[xxxix] https://www.thedailybeast.com/report-russian-hackers-had-rnc-data-but-didnt-release-it

[xl] https://gawker.com/contrary-to-dnc-claim-hacked-data-contains-a-ton-of-pe-1782132678

[xli] https://gawker.com/this-looks-like-the-dncs-hacked-trump-oppo-file-1782040426

[xlii] http://www.thesmokinggun.com/documents/crime/dnc-hacker-leaks-trump-oppo-report-647293

[xliii] https://www.buzzfeednews.com/article/kevincollier/assange-seth-rich-lies-guccifer-wikileaks-hannity

[xliv] https://themoscowproject.org/collusion/steeles-dossier-

shared-fbi/

[xlv] https://www.bbc.co.uk/news/technology-36913000

[xlvi] https://www.lawfareblog.com/rep-schiff-sen-feinstein-call-response-if-russia-behind-dnc-hack

[xlvii] https://twitter.com/realDonaldTrump/status/755551039244341253

[xlviii] https://www.npr.org/2019/04/19/714890832/mueller-report-raises-new-questions-about-russias-hacking-targets-in-2016?t=1560623987758

[xlix] https://www.washingtonpost.com/news/the-switch/wp/2016/07/22/wikileaks-posts-nearly-20000-hacked-dnc-emails-online/

[l] https://www.theguardian.com/us-news/2016/jul/24/debbie-wasserman-schultz-resigns-dnc-chair-emails-sanders

[li] https://www.theguardian.com/us-news/2016/jul/24/clinton-campaign-blames-russia-wikileaks-sanders-dnc-emails

[lii] https://twitter.com/realDonaldTrump/status/758335147183788032

[liii] https://www.vanityfair.com/news/2019/03/trump-russia-emails-joke-cpac-speech

[liv] https://www.vanityfair.com/news/2016/07/donald-trump-russia-hack-hillary-clinton-email

[lv] https://www.nbcnews.com/storyline/2016-conventions/hillary-clinton-becomes-first-female-nominee-major-u-s-political-n617406

[lvi] https://www.washingtonexaminer.com/opinion/bernies-promised-land

[lvii] https://www.vox.com/policy-and-politics/2017/11/14/16640082/donna-brazile-warren-bernie-sanders-democratic-primary-rigged

[lviii] https://www.theguardian.com/commentisfree/2018/jun/11/democrat-primary-elections-need-reform

[lix] https://www.bbc.co.uk/news/world-us-canada-41850798

[lx] https://www.nytimes.com/2018/05/16/us/politics/crossfire-hurricane-trump-russia-fbi-mueller-investigation.html

[lxi] https://www.motherjones.com/politics/2018/03/why-the-hell-are-we-standing-down/

[lxii] https://www.forbes.com/sites/thomasbrewster/2016/08/15/twitter-wordpress-guccifer-censoring-hacker/

[lxiii] https://www.nbcnews.com/news/us-news/fbi-warned-trump-2016-russians-would-try-infiltrate-his-campaign-n830596

[lxiv] https://www.theguardian.com/technology/2016/aug/29/arizona-illinois-voter-registration-systems-hacked-fbi

[lxv] https://www.realclearpolitics.com/video/2016/09/09/assange_clinton_cant_be_rewarded_for_whipping_up_a_neo-mccarthyist_hysteria.html

[lxvi] https://www.businessinsider.com/mitch-mcconnell-cia-rus-sia-trump-election-2016-12?r=US&IR=T

[lxvii] https://www.washingtonpost.com/world/national-secur-ity/obama-orders-review-of-russian-hacking-during-presiden-tial-campaign/2016/12/09/31d6b300-be2a-11e6-94ac-3d324840106c_story.html?utm_term=.1350910dda26

[lxviii] https://www.foxnews.com/politics/fbi-lovers-latest-text-messages-obama-wants-to-know-everything

[lxix] https://www.politico.com/story/2016/09/carter-page-trump-conway-228641

[lxx] https://eu.usatoday.com/story/news/politics/2016/09/28/fbi-hackers-voter-databases-comey/91222454/

[lxxi] https://www.vox.com/world/2018/1/30/16951490/trump-russia-dossier-cody-shearer-memo-nunes

[lxxii] https://www.dhs.gov/news/2016/10/07/joint-statement-department-homeland-security-and-office-director-national

[lxxiii] https://www.bbc.co.uk/news/world-us-canada-37639370

[lxxiv] https://www.nytimes.com/2016/10/08/us/politics/hillary-clinton-speeches-wikileaks.html

[lxxv] https://www.washingtonpost.com/news/the-fix/wp/2016/10/19/the-final-trump-clinton-debate-transcript-an-notated/?utm_term=.5cacfcda8e84

[lxxvi] https://dailycaller.com/2018/03/31/debunking-hillary-17-intelligence-agencies-claim/

[lxxvii] https://www.vanityfair.com/news/2017/02/james-comey-fbi-director-letter

[lxxviii] https://www.newsweek.com/hillary-clinton-emails-fake-news-618557

[lxxix] https://www.brandwatch.com/blog/react-but-her-emails/

[lxxx] https://www.realclearpolitics.com/video/2017/12/04/cnn_fbi_agent_strzok_changed_comeys_clinton_language_from_grossly_negligent_to_extremely_careless.html

[lxxxi] https://www.politico.com/story/2016/10/reid-comey-let-ter-230514

[lxxxii] https://www.politico.com/story/2016/10/obama-administration-accuses-russian-government-of-election-year-hacking-229296

[lxxxiii] https://edition.cnn.com/2016/10/12/politics/florida-elec-tion-hack/index.html

[lxxxiv] https://techcrunch.com/2019/04/18/russia-hackers-flor-ida-elections/

[lxxxv] https://www.independent.co.uk/news/world/americas/dnc-hack-russia-republican-democrat-bugged-headquarters-washington-watergate-a7398626.html

[lxxxvi] https://www.motherjones.com/politics/2016/11/dnc-told-fbi-it-may-have-been-bugged/

[lxxxvii] https://www.motherjones.com/politics/2016/11/dnc-told-fbi-it-may-have-been-bugged/

[lxxxviii] https://www.foxnews.com/politics/clintons-deplorables-gaffe-touches-off-merch-meme-frenzy

[lxxxix] https://www.theguardian.com/us-news/2017/jan/10/fbi-chief-given-dossier-by-john-mccain-alleging-secret-trump-russia-contacts

[xc] https://www.politico.com/story/2016/12/trump-team-russia-cia-intel-election-232460

[xci] https://eu.usatoday.com/story/news/politics/onpolitics/2016/12/16/clinton-blames-putin-personal-beef-election-plot/95522154/

[xcii] https://www.euronews.com/2016/12/16/not-much-happens-in-russia-without-putin-obama-on-russian-us-election-hack

[xciii] https://www.treasury.gov/resource-center/sanctions/Programs/Documents/cyber2_eo.pdf

[xciv] https://www.us-cert.gov/sites/default/files/publications/JAR_16-20296A_GRIZZLY%20STEPPE-2016-1229.pdf

[xcv] https://wikileaks.org/ciav7p1/

[xcvi] https://wikileaks.org/ciav7p1/#FAQ

[xcvii] https://www.nytimes.com/2016/12/30/world/europe/russia-diplomats-us-hacking.html

[xcviii] https://twitter.com/realDonaldTrump/status/814919370711461890

[xcix] https://www.vanityfair.com/news/2016/12/twitter-meltsdown-after-donald-trump-praises-putin

[c] https://twitter.com/kharyp/status/831702885637423104

[ci] https://twitter.com/peterdaou/status/814930146255892480

[cii] https://twitter.com/EvanMcMullin/status/814928592559689728

[ciii] https://twitter.com/Weinsteinlaw/sta-

tus/1021177663854137344

[civ] https://www.voanews.com/usa/top-us-intelligence-officials-brief-obama-senate-russia-hacking

[cv] https://www.dni.gov/files/documents/ICA_2017_01.pdf